"Having spent decades advising growing compani
finance, and strategic matters—first as a practicing attorney and then
as co-founder of OutsideGC—I understand the critical role that sound
financial management plays in business success. William Lieberman has
created an invaluable resource that demystifies finance for CEOs who need
to make smart decisions but don't have the luxury of a full-time CFO.
'*The No-BS Financial Playbook for Small Business CEOs*' combines
deep expertise with practical wisdom that every entrepreneur can apply
immediately."

— **Bill Stone**
Strategic Advisor, The CEO's Right Hand

"As someone who built and scaled a digital marketing agency from startup
to a successful private equity exit, I can tell you that mastering the financial
side of your business is absolutely critical—and it's where most entrepreneurs struggle. William's book fills that gap perfectly.

Having been in EO with William for years, I've witnessed his deep
expertise in helping companies navigate the financial complexities of scaling. This playbook distills decades of real-world experience into actionable
strategies that every growth-focused CEO needs to understand.

From managing cash flow during rapid growth to preparing your
financials for investor scrutiny, William covers the essential financial fundamentals that can make or break a scaling business. William covers all
the topics I wish I'd had as I launched and grew my firm—it would have
saved me countless headaches.

If you're serious about building a scalable, valuable company, '*The
No-BS Financial Playbook for Small Business CEOs*' isn't just recommended reading—it's required reading."

— **Ben Kirshner**
Founder & Former CEO, Tinuiti

"Having scaled 1-800-GOT-JUNK? to over 3,100 employees systemwide as COO, I know firsthand that rapid growth without proper financial infrastructure is a recipe for disaster. William Lieberman's '*The No-BS Financial Playbook for Small Business CEOs*' provides the financial roadmap that every scaling company desperately needs.

Most entrepreneurs are visionaries who can sell and build, but they often lack the financial acumen to support explosive growth. I've seen too many promising companies crumble under the weight of their success because they didn't have the cash flow management, financial controls, and reporting systems in place to handle scale.

William's book fills this critical gap with practical, battle-tested strategies. From building your finance team at the right stages to preparing for capital raises and exits, this playbook gives CEOs the financial confidence to scale without fear. The frameworks he provides aren't just theory—they're proven systems that can handle real-world growth challenges.

Every CEO should read this book, and ensure their COO reads it too. Financial mastery isn't optional when you're scaling—it's the foundation that makes everything else possible."

— **Cameron Herold**
Former COO, 1-800-GOT-JUNK?; Founder, COO Alliance

"If you, the CEO of an SMB, were asked to rate your own competence in financial management on a scale of 1-5 and your number is 3 or lower, then '*The No-BS Financial Playbook for Small Business CEOs*' is a must-read. It explains concepts in plain language, shows you how to build a scalable financial infrastructure, and delivers actionable insights based on real-world experience."

— **Jeannette Hobson**
Chair, Vistage International

"As the founder of both a bookkeeping firm and a SaaS company serving accounting practices, I work daily with businesses at every stage of financial maturity. William Lieberman's '*The No-BS Financial Playbook for Small Business CEOs*' addresses the critical gap I see repeatedly: CEOs who are brilliant operators but lack the financial frameworks to scale effectively.

Through Creative Business, Inc., I've worked with hundreds of growing companies, and the pattern is always the same—businesses hit growth plateaus not because of market issues or operational problems, but because they lack proper financial infrastructure. William's book provides the roadmap these companies desperately need.

What sets this playbook apart is its practical focus on building scalable systems. From establishing the right finance team structure to implementing controls that grow with your business, William provides specific, actionable guidance based on real entrepreneurial experience. This isn't academic theory—it's battle-tested wisdom from someone who has built, scaled, and successfully exited companies.

Every accounting professional should recommend this book to their growth-stage clients, and every CEO should read it before they hit the financial growing pains that derail so many promising businesses. The financial foundations William outlines aren't just nice-to-have—they're essential infrastructure for any company serious about scaling."

— **Jeanne Hardy**
Founder, Creative Business Inc. & Levvy

"As a CEO who has led multiple companies and served on William's board at Xtiva Financial Systems, I've experienced both sides of the financial management challenge: implementing these systems as an operator and evaluating them as a board member. William's '*The No-BS Financial Playbook for Small Business CEOs*' captures the essential financial disciplines that separate successful scaling companies from those that struggle.

What sets William apart is his ability to build financial infrastructure that actually supports growth rather than constraining it. During my time on Xtiva's board, I watched him navigate complex fundraising processes, implement financial controls, and create the reporting systems that gave us the confidence to help guide the company.

Too many CEOs treat financial management as a necessary evil rather than a strategic advantage. This book shows you how to flip that mindset and use financial excellence as a competitive weapon. From cash flow forecasting to investor relations, William provides the frameworks that enable CEOs to make confident, data-driven decisions.

Having seen these principles work in practice, I can tell you they're not just sound theory—they're the financial foundation that allows visionary leaders to execute on their biggest ambitions without getting derailed by avoidable financial pitfalls."

— Michele McGovern
Former CEO & Board Member
Board Member, Xtiva Financial Systems

The No-BS Financial Playbook for Small Business CEOs

How to Create a Scalable and Valuable Company

William Lieberman
Founder & Managing Partner

Amy Wright
Director of Content Marketing

The
CEO's
RIGHT HAND ®
Outsourced Finance & Accounting Services

PERFORMANCE PUBLISHING

First Edition: July 2025

The CEO's Right Hand
265 Sunrise Highway, Suite 1-779
Rockville Centre, NY 11570
www.tcrh.co

Illustrations by: Carrie Segal

DISCLAIMER: The information contained in this book is meant for informational purposes only. The author and publisher are not engaged in rendering legal, accounting, or other professional services through this book. If expert assistance is required, the services of a competent professional should be sought. The author and publisher shall not be liable for any loss or damage caused directly or indirectly by the information contained in this book. Select sections of this work were drafted and/or developed with the assistance of artificial intelligence tools.

ISBN:
978-1-967451-99-9 paperback
978-1-967451-16-6 paperback (color)
978-1-967451-14-2 hardcover (color)
978-1-967451-15-9 ebook

CONTENTS

INTRODUCTION

What Is This Book About?

Entrepreneurs, founders and CEOs share a common drive: to build something meaningful, scale it and create wealth—not just for themselves, but for their teams and investors. But building a business is hard. There's a reason people say it takes 10 years to become an "overnight success." Behind every win are years of struggle, setbacks and relentless effort. Most people only see the success, not the work that went into it. Unlike the outward façade, being a business owner is one of the hardest jobs out there. (Believe me—I have been there!)

Founders are great at creating things but (and this is a vast generalization) not as good at the "blocking and tackling" needed to create a truly scalable and profitable company. What I mean when I say "scalable" is that the company's revenues are growing faster than the operating expenses. That's the goal.

The phrase "economies of scale" is what all founders are looking to achieve when they look to grow their companies. *But how do you do that when you don't have any experience? And what are the key components on which you should focus? How do you even measure success?*

This book gives founders and CEOs financial tools to build a scalable, profitable company. If you don't have a CFO, it will help you manage finances effectively. If you do, it will help you ask the right questions to ensure financial success.

Why I Chose to Write This Book

There are plenty of "self-help" books out there that will teach you finance or accounting. But most are not geared towards the small business CEO, or do not have practical, take-away learning lessons from someone who has been in the trenches just like you. This book changes that.

My Background

To give you context, here is how my entrepreneurial journey started and where it led me 40+ years later.

While in college, I launched my first company, Trisoft, a computer consulting and software firm. This was the mid-1980s when PCs were just emerging. I helped small and mid-sized businesses navigate this new technology—buying, configuring and using early spreadsheet programs like VisiCalc. At the time, the entire World Wide Web (what we now all call "the Internet") consisted of just 400 websites (today, there are more than 1.1 billion).

After running Trisoft for a year post-graduation, I went back to earn my MBA and MS in Computer Science. During a summer break, I worked at Shearson, building analytics for an investment management platform. That led to a job on Wall Street in investment banking at Bankers Trust, where I managed a global tech rollout before shifting to M&A.

Not long after, I reconnected with my former Shearson manager, and we launched Capital Markets Research (CMR), a financial analytics company. We started small. I lived with my parents, eating Cup O' Noodles daily to make ends meet. Eventually, we grew, relocated to San Francisco and built out a full finance and technology team.

While running CMR, I met Tom Moysak, co-founder of a broker-dealer firm in New York. He needed software to manage commissions, and we built a custom solution called Commission Manager. His clearing firm, Bear Stearns, saw the product's potential, leading to the birth of my next venture: Xtiva Financial Systems.

In 1998, I co-founded Xtiva with my longtime business partner, James Iacabucci. We started scrappy, running operations out of James'

San Francisco apartment, with our "server" literally sitting under his dining room table. I managed sales, marketing, finance, accounting and even customer support. Meanwhile, James built the software, one of the first SaaS products in the financial services industry (long before SaaS was a common term).

We grew quickly. Tom Moysak and his business partner invested $550,000, allowing us to move into an office in Union Square, hire a team and accelerate growth. Within a few years, we hit $2M in annual recurring revenues (ARR). At that point, we needed more capital to scale.

I led our first major fundraising round, securing $1M in equity from friends and family. Later, we raised $3.5M in Series A from ADP Brokerage (now Broadridge). That capital fueled expansion, a stronger management team and major enterprise deals, including a $1.2M contract with MetLife Securities, a significant leap from our initial $395/month pricing model.

Then came 2007–2008; the financial crisis hit. Lehman Brothers and Bear Stearns collapsed. At the same time, I went through a grueling six-year divorce that eventually went to trial. I stepped back from the CEO role to focus on finance and investor relations, staying with Xtiva for another six years before deciding it was time for a change.

In 2014, I sold my stake in Xtiva and joined Interactive Donor, a SaaS startup in the nonprofit space. My job? Launch the product and secure funding. After six months and $200,000 of my own money, I realized the business model wasn't viable. I shut it down and moved on. (Thankfully, I got 50% credit on my taxes for the lost investment!)

In 2015, I launched my current firm, The CEO's Right Hand ("TCRH"), as a boutique finance consulting firm. My first client was in ad tech, where I acted as a fractional CFO. From there, I leveraged my network—Entrepreneurs' Organization, Vistage, my business school alumni and 20+ years of business contacts—to grow the firm. By the end of 2015, I had multiple clients and a small team.

In 2019, I co-founded Shōri Capital, a private equity firm focused on acquiring lower middle-market companies ($10M–$30M in revenue). Over 18 months, we evaluated hundreds of businesses, bid on eight and made it to the final stages three times, but we were outbid every time by strategic buyers. After learning invaluable lessons from the "buy-side," I closed the firm and focused full-time on TCRH.

Over the last decade, TCRH has helped hundreds of businesses (from startups to middle-market firms) raise capital, scale and exit successfully. I've seen what works, what doesn't and what every CEO must get right to build a scalable, profitable and valuable business.

Examples of What Can Go Wrong

In my 30+ years of working with businesses, I've seen plenty of mistakes—some minor, others catastrophic. Many could have been avoided with better financial planning and execution. Here are a few real-world examples.

The $9M Marketing Firm That Lost a Deal Over Bad Books

A marketing firm generating $9 million in annual revenue was in negotiations to sell. However, the buyer couldn't make sense of their financials because they didn't follow a proper revenue recognition policy.

They were recording revenue on a cash basis (when payments came in) instead of an accrual basis (when services were actually provided). With so many transactions, their books were a mess, and the buyer walked away.

It took months of costly cleanup to get their financials in order before they could re-enter the market.

Key Lesson: Buyers need clear, accurate financials. Without them, your business is worth less—or nothing at all.

The CEO Who Ignored Financial Warnings

We worked with a small professional services firm whose CEO was spending recklessly. For nine months, our team provided weekly cash flow forecasts showing exactly when they'd run out of money.

The CEO ignored every warning. He kept spending without securing outside capital, wasn't landing new customers and was even using company funds for personal expenses (totaling tens of thousands of dollars).

By the time we stepped away, the company was on life support.

Key Lesson: If your finance team says you're running out of cash, listen before it's too late.

The Startup That Hired Too Fast

A startup CEO was confident huge sales were coming, so he hired ahead of revenue, despite our repeated warnings.

But the expected sales never materialized. The company burned through cash, couldn't raise outside capital and had to cut staff, in a panic. Today, it's barely hanging on.

Key Lesson: Hope isn't a strategy. Hire based on actual revenue, not wishful projections.

My Own Fundraising Mistake at Xtiva

I've made mistakes, too. When raising Xtiva's Series A, I trusted an investment banker who insisted we only pursue ADP as an investor, convinced we'd get a great deal.

We didn't. With just two weeks of cash left, we had zero leverage and had to accept less-than-ideal terms.

Key Lesson: Never rely on a single funding source. Always have multiple investors in play to maintain negotiating power.

The Bottom Line

Many CEOs are great at sales, product development or customer service, but finance isn't their strength. The smartest ones recognize their blind spots and get help early before financial mistakes derail their business.

Who Should Be Reading This Book

This book is for founders, entrepreneurs and CEOs of small businesses who want to better understand finance and accounting to effectively grow, scale and eventually exit their company. When I say, "small businesses," I mean those with less than $50 million in revenues, whether you're a startup or an established business looking to strengthen your financial foundation.

This book is particularly useful for U.S.-based companies selling products or services in B2B (business-to-business) or D2C (direct-to-consumer) markets. To help you assess your financial readiness, I've included a self-assessment quiz with key questions every CEO should be able to answer. These questions highlight common challenges business leaders face and why financial strategy matters in scaling a company successfully.

The Quiz

Instructions: Read through each question and answer Yes or No. As a second mental step, ask yourself if you know where in your financial data or other reports you would look to find the data required to support your answer in a real-world scenario. If you feel confident, check Yes. Sum your number of Yes answers at the bottom of the quiz. If you answer No to a question, read through our advice for how to arrive at a "Yes" in the following pages.

	YES	NO
01. Are you confident in your ability to fund your business for the next 6-12 months?		
02. Do you know how to increase cash flow for your business?		
03. Do you know how much capital you need for the next 12 months?		
04. Does your team have the expertise you require to raise capital?		
05. Are you confident that you can sell potential investors on your vision?		
06. Do you have an idea as to how much your company is worth?		
07. Do you know the key performance indicators (KPIs) for your company?		
08. Are your financial reports insightful enough to guide your decisions?		
09. Do you have a financial forecast that provides clear visibility into the next 12 months?		
10. Does your finance and accounting staff have the skills you need to take your business to the next level?		
11. Do you have either a part-time or full-time CFO on your team?		

Total "Yes" Answers ▶

Answer Key

0-2	3-5	6-9	10-11

What Will You Get Out of It

This book is designed to be a practical guide; therefore, I have included real examples so that you can see the impact of building the proper financial infrastructure from the beginning. Each chapter breaks down financial concepts in a way that is easy to understand and apply (even if you don't have a background in finance). By reading this book, you will:

Gain clarity on key financial principles. You'll learn how to build a financial foundation that supports growth, stability and long-term success.

Avoid costly mistakes. Many businesses struggle or fail due to preventable financial missteps. This book shares real-world examples of what can go wrong and how to avoid those pitfalls.

Improve cash flow and profitability. You'll discover strategies to optimize cash flow, manage expenses and ensure your company remains financially healthy.

Make informed, strategic decisions. With a solid understanding of financial management, you'll be able to plan for the future with confidence and make data-driven decisions.

Communicate effectively with financial professionals. Whether you have a CFO or are managing finances on your own, this book will help you ask the right questions, interpret financial data and work more effectively with investors, lenders and advisors.

Build a scalable business. You'll learn how to structure your finances so that your revenue grows faster than your expenses, allowing you to scale efficiently.

This book is filled with actionable insights, step-by-step guidance and tools to help you take control of your company's financial future. Whether you're just starting out or leading an established business, you'll walk away with the knowledge you need to create a more profitable and sustainable company.

As you dive into the strategies ahead, you'll discover I've packed this book with practical tools you can use immediately. Rather than cramming everything between these covers, I've created a digital companion with all the templates, checklists, and resources mentioned throughout. Visit https://theceosrighthand.co/books/financial-playbook/resource-hub/ or scan the QR code below to access your complete toolkit.

About the Authors

William Lieberman

William Lieberman is the Founder and Managing Partner of The CEO's Right Hand, a New York-based consulting firm providing comprehensive strategic, financial, and operational advice to founders, CEOs, and executive teams.

With over 30 years of entrepreneurial experience, William has built, scaled, and sold multiple successful businesses across diverse industries. His career spans roles as Chairman, CEO, CFO, and trusted advisor, giving him a unique perspective on the challenges business leaders face at every stage of growth.

William's entrepreneurial journey began in the 1980s when he launched Trisoft, a computer consulting and software firm, while still in college. After earning his BS in Computer Engineering from UC San Diego and dual Masters degrees in Business Administration and Computer Science from UCLA, he worked at Bankers Trust in investment banking before co-founding Capital Markets Research (CMR), a financial analytics company.

In 1998, William co-founded Xtiva Financial Systems, a financial technology company that grew from startup to over $10 million in revenue with 100+ clients. Under his leadership, Xtiva made the Inc. 500/5000 list three times and the Deloitte & Touche Fast 50 ranking. He successfully led multiple capital raises, including a Series A round from a Fortune 100 strategic investor, and secured multimillion-dollar enterprise contracts with major financial institutions.

After selling his stake in Xtiva in 2014, William founded The CEO's Right Hand, which has since helped hundreds of businesses raise capital, scale successfully, and achieve profitable exits. His firm specializes in providing fractional CFO, M&A advisory & HR consulting to small and mid-sized companies.

The firm's approach combines deep financial expertise with practical operational experience, allowing the team to translate complex financial concepts into actionable strategies for business leaders. As "quick studies" who can immediately grasp the fundamental drivers in any business model, his team helps CEOs build the infrastructure necessary for sustainable growth while avoiding costly financial missteps.

Throughout his career, William has demonstrated that proper financial management is not merely about tracking numbers—it's about creating a foundation for strategic decision-making that drives long-term business success.

Amy Wright

Amy Wright is an experienced marketing professional who helps businesses connect with customers by developing and executing content marketing strategies that build their reputations and increase online visibility. She drives traffic and generates leads across industries by planning, creating, and promoting highly targeted quality content that educates, informs, and addresses customer concerns.

Amy has been marketing solutions to various audiences, from businesses to consumers to educators, for over 20 years, contributing to the success of fledgling startups and large global organizations. She currently focuses on developing and promoting written digital content for small-to-medium-sized service-based organizations, collaborating with each firm's subject matter experts to craft content that demonstrates their expertise and promotes solutions.

Amy is an expert in search engine optimization (SEO) and applies those skills to her work—giving each piece of content its best chance of success while also managing the firm's website and overall online presence, ensuring its entire digital footprint supports the effort. In prior roles, she was responsible for social media marketing, analyst relations, partner programs, market research, and competitive analysis.

Amy earned a Bachelor of Science in Business Administration with an emphasis in Marketing, an Associate Degree in Computer Information Systems, and multiple industry-related certifications. She lives in California and spends her free time with family and friends, engaged with local community organizations, hiking, and reading.

About The CEO's Right Hand

The CEO's Right Hand (TCRH) is a comprehensive outsourced finance and human resources consulting firm serving early-stage growth companies. We bridge the gap between the need for executive-level expertise and the challenge of affording full-time C-suite talent by providing fractional services that deliver high-caliber leadership at a fraction of the cost.

Our services are built around four core offerings:

1. **Fractional CFO Services:** We provide strategic financial leadership, including financial reporting and analysis, cash flow management, forecasting and strategic planning. Our CFO services help companies build the infrastructure needed to scale while providing actionable insights into critical business decisions.
2. **Fractional HR & Talent Services:** Our HR team delivers executive-level expertise in organizational design, compliance, talent acquisition and development. We help companies build and maintain high-performing teams while ensuring proper infrastructure for growth.
3. **Capital Raising & Strategic Advisory:** Having raised billions in equity and debt financing, our team guides companies through the entire capital raising process, from strategic planning through deal execution. We also provide exit planning and M&A advisory services.
4. **Accounting & Bookkeeping:** We ensure businesses maintain accurate financial records and reporting through comprehensive accounting services, including monthly financials, budget support and accounts management.

What sets us apart is our team's firsthand experience as entrepreneurs and business operators. We've built, managed and sold businesses ourselves, giving us a unique understanding of the challenges our clients face. This experience allows us to provide practical, implementation-focused solutions rather than just theoretical advice.

For growing companies looking to build a strong financial and operational foundation, The CEO's Right Hand offers the strategic guidance and hands-on support needed to achieve sustainable growth and success. **For more information, please visit us at <u>www.tcrh.co</u>.** You can also email me at william@tcrh.co.

PART 1

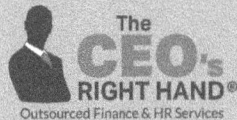

Laying the Financial Foundation

CHAPTER 1

Understanding Financial Management

What is Financial Management?

Financial management is a critical function for any small business. As CEO, you play a central role in ensuring the company's finances are structured for growth and stability. Whether or not you have a CFO or financial team, you must understand key financial principles to make informed decisions, minimize risk and drive success.

Why Financial Management Matters for CEOs

- **Guiding Strategic Growth** – A clear understanding of your company's financial health enables you to identify opportunities, mitigate risks and make smarter decisions that directly impact profitability. Without financial oversight, CEOs may unknowingly steer their businesses toward cash flow problems, inefficient spending or unsustainable growth.
- **Building Trust with Stakeholders** – Investors, lenders and board members rely on accurate, timely financial insights to gauge the business's viability. A CEO who understands financial data can confidently communicate with stakeholders, secure funding and establish long-term credibility.
- **Measuring Success & Adjusting Course** – Tracking key financial metrics such as revenue growth, profit margins and cash flow trends helps CEOs assess what's working, what's not and when to pivot. Without regular financial analysis, businesses risk stagnation or financial mismanagement.

Many small business CEOs excel at sales, product development or operations but struggle with financial management. They assume profitability means their business is financially sound, that is, until a cash shortfall, tax issue or investor concern forces them to confront their numbers.

The goal of this book is to help you take control of your company's financial health, whether you're managing finances yourself or working with a CFO. By prioritizing financial management, you can build a scalable, profitable business with long-term sustainability.

The Team

There are many different roles needed to run the finances of a business. How many people you need and what roles they will fill depends on the size, stage and complexity of your firm. A small retail store may only need a single part-time bookkeeper while a $50 million manufacturer of electronic components may need a full team. For the most part, small businesses are too small to afford or frankly even need full-time staff. That's when CEOs turn to fractional finance and accounting resources to provide the needed leadership and execution on a part-time basis.

The team you have, whether it's just a couple of people or a team of 20, or 200, needs to have some sort of leader at the helm. When you are just starting, you, as the CEO, will often have to play the role of the senior finance lead as well. However, as you get to $1 million in revenues, things begin to get more complicated and the need for expert guidance becomes critical. Thus, the need arises for a Chief Financial Officer (CFO).

How Can a Chief Financial Officer Help?

In small businesses, the Chief Financial Officer plays a crucial role in ensuring the financial health and success of the company. The CFO is responsible for overseeing all financial activities, including budgeting, forecasting, financial analysis and reporting. They work closely with the CEO and other members of the executive team to develop and implement financial strategies that support the company's goals and objectives.

One of the key responsibilities of the CFO in a small business is to provide accurate and timely financial information to the CEO and other stakeholders. This information is essential for making informed decisions about the company's operations, investments and overall financial health. The CFO must ensure that financial data is accurate, reliable and up to date so that the CEO can clearly understand the company's financial position.

In addition to providing financial information, the CFO is also responsible for developing and implementing financial policies and procedures that help to improve the company's financial performance. This may include developing budgets, cash flow projections and financial forecasts, as well as monitoring and analyzing key financial metrics to identify areas for improvement. By working closely with the CEO, the CFO can help to identify opportunities for growth and profitability, as well as potential risks that may impact the company's financial health.

Another key role of the CFO in a small business is managing the company's financial resources effectively. This includes overseeing the company's accounting and finance functions and managing relationships with banks, lenders and other financial institutions. The CFO must also ensure compliance with financial regulations and reporting requirements and work to minimize financial risks that could impact the company's operations.

Overall, the CFO plays a critical role in the success of a small business by providing financial leadership and guidance to the CEO and other members of the executive team. By working closely with the CEO to develop and implement financial strategies to support the company's goals and objectives, the CFO helps to ensure the company's long-term financial health and success. CEOs of small businesses should recognize the importance of having a strong CFO in place to help drive the financial success of their company.

Fractional CFOs

Most small firms cannot afford to hire a full-time CFO or simply do not need a permanent person in that role. For example, if you have a $3 million professional services firm that is growing nicely, there is no reason to bring on a full-time CFO to help guide you. But that does not mean you should try and go it alone without any outside expert advice.

You can achieve that same guidance from a fractional (what used to be called "part-time") finance executive who will spend a portion of their time with you on a regular basis. This could be one day a week or sometimes, even less. It all depends on the complexity of your business and what strategic initiatives you are undertaking or plan to complete in the coming 12–24 months.

Tool: You can compare the cost of a full-time CFO with a fractional (part-time) one using this calculator that we developed: *https://theceosrighthand.co/resources/fractional-cfo-cost-calculator/*

AI Tip

Use AI-powered financial dashboards that automatically pull data from multiple systems to give you real-time visibility into your company's financial health. Instead of waiting for monthly reports, you can make informed decisions based on current data, allowing you to spot trends and address issues before they impact performance.

Key Takeaways

- **Informed CEOs make smarter decisions.** A solid grasp of financial management enables CEOs to drive business success with confidence.

- **Your team should match your business needs.** As your company grows, ensure your finance team aligns with its size, complexity and stage of growth.

- **Use fractional resources strategically.** If a full-time CFO isn't necessary or affordable yet, leverage fractional finance professionals to provide the expertise you need.

- **Strong financial leadership is non-negotiable.** A skilled CFO—full-time or fractional—acts as a trusted financial partner, guiding strategy, cash flow and growth planning.

- **A well-structured financial system is the foundation of scalability.** A CFO ensures you have the right people, data, reporting, technology and processes to support long-term success.

AI Key Takeaway Addition

Leverage AI for real-time insights. AI-powered dashboards provide continuous visibility into financial performance, enabling faster decision-making than traditional monthly reporting cycles.

Now that we have covered the CEO's role in financial management, let's explore how to build the right finance and accounting team to support your growth.

CHAPTER 2

Building Your Finance & Accounting Team

O ne of the top priorities for nearly every CEO is finding, hiring and motivating a world-class team that can make your vision a reality. After all, you can have the best products and services in the world, but if you don't have the people you need to grow and scale your business, no one will get to enjoy them. And what's the fun in that?

Many small business CEOs struggle with building their finance and accounting departments efficiently. This chapter outlines a practical approach to constructing your finance team as your company evolves, allowing you to build a capable function without breaking the bank.

Understanding Team Evolution

If you think of your company as a living, breathing organism, it's easy to liken its growth to that of a human being. For example, imagine any productive adult you know. They didn't start off that way. Instead, they began life as an infant—picking up skills, relying on help from their elders, experiencing setbacks and building confidence until, at some point, they were ready to move out into the world as a self-sufficient adult.

Your finance and accounting organization will experience a similar journey. When you are just starting, you will rely upon your wits, a patchwork of skills and advice from your network. But before too long, you will be ready to hire. And when that time comes, I recommend starting from the bottom. Pull in the well-qualified, but least expensive, resources first and use fractional (part-time) help at the higher levels. Then, as you grow, you can begin to specialize and commit to full-time employees.

Let's look at the positions you need to fill during each phase. In the following pages, we describe five key roles companies need and the external constituents you might enlist for various aspects of your business. This list of roles is by no means exhaustive, but it should give you a sense of the skills you will seek over time. Before we dive in, however, let us set the stage from a big-picture perspective.

Each organization combines these roles differently, so there is some overlap in responsibilities to allow for specialization as your business grows. However, we find it helps to consider each function's point of view (time horizon). For example, below are the positions we cover and their respective viewpoints:

ROLE	VIEWPOINT
Full-Charge Bookkeeper	What is happening *today*?
Accounting Manager	What is happening *this month*?
Controller	What is happening *this quarter* and *this fiscal year*?
FP&A (Financial Planning & Analysis)	What is happening in the next *1-3 years*?
Chief Financial Officer (CFO)	What happened in the *past*, what are our plans for the *future* (3-5 years out), and how should that inform decisions *today*?

The Growth-Based Staffing Approach

Although every company is unique, with different requirements based on industry and business model, most small-to-mid-sized businesses can follow a similar path for building their finance and accounting teams. Let's look at how this typically unfolds as a company grows through various revenue stages.

Less Than $2 Million in Revenue

At this earliest stage, the first hire for any finance and accounting organization will be a qualified part-time bookkeeper. This person will:

- Keep track of your transactions
- Pay bills and generate invoices
- Record incoming payments
- Manage your cash position
- Process payroll for your employees
- Reconcile books at month-end
- Generate simple financial reports
- Maintain compliance with regulatory bodies

When hiring this key person, look for someone with strong knowledge of accounting practices, proficiency with Excel, familiarity with your accounting system and keen attention to detail. A good bookkeeper will typically cost $45,000–$65,000 annually for a full-time position, but at this stage, you'll likely need them only part-time (5–10 hours per week) at an hourly rate of $40–$100.

As you continue to grow, you'll eventually encounter financial challenges beyond your bookkeeper's capabilities. For instance, you may need to raise capital to invest in research and development. Therefore, your second hire will likely be a fractional CFO. This strategic advisor will help you navigate complex financial hurdles and take over management of your finance function, including building relationships with external experts such as bankers or auditors.

A fractional CFO typically comes at a rate of $300+ per hour but may only be needed for a few hours each month at this stage. This approach gives you access to executive-level financial expertise without the $200,000+ annual salary a full-time CFO would command.

$2 Million to $5 Million in Revenue

As your business ramps up and transaction volume increases, you'll likely add a part-time accounting manager to the team. This person will:

- Manage the bookkeeper
- Close the books at month-end
- Perform higher-level accounting tasks
- Conduct light financial planning and analysis
- Report to the fractional CFO

If your bookkeeper is ready for more responsibility, you might promote them into this role and hire a new bookkeeper to handle transactional work. The accounting manager typically costs $100,000–$140,000 for a full-time position, but at this stage, a part-time arrangement at $100–$180 per hour is usually sufficient.

In most small businesses, these roles will evolve over time, with each person wearing many hats. For instance, your bookkeeper may take on some light spreadsheet work, sales administrative tasks or office management responsibilities as the business needs dictate. Eventually, their role may grow into a full-time position as transaction volume increases.

At this point, your team will be a mix consisting of:

- A full-time bookkeeper
- A part-time accounting manager (likely someone who freelances)
- A fractional CFO
- Various external constituents, such as your tax accountant

Your CFO will also begin developing the financial infrastructure you'll need to support your growing business—implementing systems, establishing processes and creating reporting frameworks that can scale with your company.

$5 Million to $10 Million in Revenue

As your business continues to grow, the demands on your team become more substantial. At this stage, you'll likely convert your part-time accounting manager into a full-time position, potentially promoting your bookkeeper if they're ready to step up.

You may also begin to specialize your team. Starting from the bottom up, you might hire part-time specialists such as:

- Accounts receivable (A/R) clerk
- Accounts payable (A/P) clerk
- Payroll clerk

These specialized positions allow your core accounting team to focus on more strategic activities rather than getting bogged down in transactional work. As transaction volume increases, these roles may eventually become full-time positions.

Your team at this stage will typically include:

- Fractional CFO
- Full-time accounting manager
- Full-time bookkeeper
- Part-time clerks handling A/R, A/P and payroll

The key advantage of this approach is its flexibility—you can adjust resource levels based on your specific needs rather than forcing yourself into traditional organizational structures that may not fit your business.

Key Finance & Accounting Roles

Let's examine the core roles that make up an effective finance and accounting team for a small business:

Full-Charge Bookkeeper

Typical cost: $45,000–$65,000 annually (full-time) or $40–$100 hourly (part-time)

When to hire: Less than $2 million in revenue

The bookkeeper focuses on what's happening *today*, handling the day-to-day financial transactions and record-keeping. They're your first line of defense against financial disorganization.

Primary responsibilities include:

- Managing daily transactions
- Processing accounts payable and receivable
- Tracking cash position
- Processing payroll
- Reconciling accounts
- Generating basic financial reports

Top qualities to look for:

- Strong knowledge of bookkeeping fundamentals
- Proficiency with accounting software
- Attention to detail and accuracy
- Organization and timeliness
- A willingness to learn and adapt as your business grows

Accounting Manager

Typical cost: $100,000–$140,000 annually (full-time) or $100–$180 hourly (part-time)

When to hire: $2 million to $5 million in revenue

The accounting manager looks at what's happening this month and quarter, overseeing accounting activities and ensuring the accuracy of your financial reporting.

Primary responsibilities include:

- Overseeing daily accounting operations
- Performing quality assurance on financial data
- Preparing financial statements
- Coordinating with tax accountants and auditors
- Developing accounting policies and procedures
- Managing the bookkeeper and accounting clerks

Top qualities to look for:

- Deep knowledge of accounting principles
- Experience with month-end closing processes
- Management capability
- Strong analytical skills
- Ability to implement and improve processes

Controller

Typical cost: $130,000–$210,000 annually (full-time) or $150–$250 hourly (part-time)

When to hire: $10 million+ in revenue

The controller takes a longer view, looking at what's happening this quarter and fiscal year. They take ownership of the entire accounting function, ensuring accuracy and compliance while building scalable systems.

Primary responsibilities include:

- Overseeing all accounting operations
- Creating internal controls and processes
- Managing budgeting and forecasting
- Auditing historical financials
- Preparing financial statements
- Managing the accounting team
- Building relationships with financial partners

Top qualities to look for:

- Extensive knowledge of accounting standards and regulations
- Experience with auditing and compliance
- Strategic thinking and problem-solving skills
- Team leadership abilities
- Experience with financial systems implementation

Financial Planning & Analysis (FP&A)

Typical cost: $140,000–$175,000 annually (full-time) or $125–$250 hourly (part-time)

When to hire: $10 million+ in revenue

The FP&A role takes a forward-looking perspective, analyzing data to understand what will happen in the next 1–3 years. This position bridges the gap between accounting (historical data) and strategic decision-making.

Primary responsibilities include:

- Leading budgeting and forecasting processes
- Building financial models
- Analyzing proposed initiatives
- Identifying operational improvements
- Tracking performance against goals
- Providing insights to drive strategic decisions

Top qualities to look for:

- Advanced Excel and modeling skills
- Strong analytical capabilities
- Ability to translate complex data into actionable insights
- Business acumen and strategic thinking
- Clear communication skills

Chief Financial Officer (CFO)

Typical cost: $250,000–$350,000+ annually (full-time) or $300+ hourly (part-time)

When to hire: Fractional at less than $2 million; full-time at $25 million+

The CFO takes the broadest view, considering what happened in the past, planning for the future and determining how this view should inform decisions today.

Primary responsibilities include:

- Providing strategic financial guidance
- Leading capital raising activities
- Developing growth strategies and plans
- Overseeing the finance and accounting function
- Building relationships with investors and financial partners
- Identifying and mitigating financial risks
- Supporting major business decisions with financial analysis

Top qualities to look for:

- Strategic thinking and business partnership skills
- Experience relevant to your specific needs (e.g., capital raising)
- Track record of driving profitable growth
- Strong leadership and communication abilities
- Ability to translate financial insights into business strategy

---

Resource: The Financial Executives Networking Group (The FENG) is a membership group of more than 36,000 finance executives, including CFOs and Controllers across the U.S. and internationally. You can post job listings and find very qualified candidates using their help. Go to www.thefeng.org for more information.

The Fractional Approach

For small businesses, a full-time CFO and specialized staff aren't always necessary or financially feasible. This is where fractional resources become invaluable.

A fractional resource is essentially a part-time executive or specialist who works with multiple clients, giving each the benefit of their expertise without the full-time cost. The "tipping point" for converting a fractional position to full-time is typically around 50% utilization, or whenever it's no longer cost-effective to continue with a part-time arrangement.

Benefits of the fractional approach include:

1. **Cost efficiency:** Access to high-level expertise at a fraction of the full-time cost
2. **Flexibility:** Ability to scale hours up or down based on business needs
3. **Experience:** Fractional executives typically bring diverse experience from working with multiple companies
4. **Objectivity:** External perspective can identify issues that insiders might miss
5. **Network:** Access to the fractional executive's professional network

Most small businesses can leverage this approach effectively until they reach $25 million+ in revenue, at which point the complexity and volume of financial activities often justify full-time executive leadership.

Building Your External Network

Beyond your internal team, you'll need relationships with external financial partners who provide specialized expertise. These include:

Tax Accountant

Every company needs a tax accountant to ensure compliance with applicable tax laws and file returns on your behalf. A good tax accountant will also help with tax planning to minimize your tax burden. Establish this relationship early and provide your financial data at least one month before tax deadlines.

External Auditors

If you plan to raise capital, sell or merge your company, you'll need an external auditing firm. These professionals examine your books to ensure GAAP compliance and accuracy, providing an independent verification that increases stakeholder confidence. Start this relationship at least one year before any planned capital event.

Tip: If someone asks you for your "audited financials" and you do not have a regular audit performed annually, see if they will accept a "review" instead of an "audit." Reviews are significantly less expensive and cover most of the same details as an audit.

Bankers

Establish a relationship with a commercial banker before you need financing. This makes it easier to secure credit lines or loans when the need arises. Your banker should understand your business model and growth plans to serve as an effective financial partner.

Wealth Advisors

As your company grows, you'll likely need to implement retirement plans for employees. A wealth advisor can help set up the proper plan structure, educate employees and ensure compliance with regulations.

Key Hiring Considerations

When building your finance team, consider these factors to ensure you're making the right decisions:

1. **Scalability:** Hire people who can grow with your business or who understand their role is transitional as the company evolves.
2. **Cultural fit:** Finance team members must align with your company values and work effectively with other departments.
3. **Technical vs. strategic skills:** Balance technical accounting expertise with strategic financial thinking based on your current stage.
4. **Industry experience:** For certain sectors (like SaaS, manufacturing or healthcare), industry-specific accounting knowledge can be extremely valuable.

5. **Systems knowledge:** Look for familiarity with the accounting and financial systems you use or plan to implement.
6. **Growth mindset:** Small business environments change rapidly—team members should be adaptable and eager to learn.

Implementation Timeline

A typical finance team implementation timeline might look like this:

Startup Phase (Pre-revenue to $1 million)

- CEO handles basic financial tasks
- Engage external tax accountant
- Establish banking relationship
- Consider part-time bookkeeper (5–10 hours/week)

Early Growth ($1 million to $2 million)

- Committed part-time bookkeeper
- Engage fractional CFO (4–8 hours/month)
- Implement proper accounting system
- Develop initial financial reporting

Expansion ($2 million to $5 million)

- Full-time bookkeeper
- Part-time accounting manager
- Fractional CFO (8–16 hours/month)
- Develop financial planning process
- Establish basic financial controls

Scaling ($5 million to $10 million)

- Full-time accounting manager
- Specialized part-time clerks (A/P, A/R, Payroll)
- Fractional CFO (16–32 hours/month)

- Comprehensive reporting package (monthly/quarterly)
- Robust budgeting and forecasting

Maturity ($10 million to $25 million)

- Controller (full or part-time)
- FP&A specialist (part-time)
- Departmentalized finance function
- Advanced financial systems
- Strategic financial planning

AI Tip

Before hiring additional accounting staff, evaluate AI automation tools that can handle routine tasks like data entry, invoice processing, and basic reconciliations. One AI solution might eliminate the need for a full-time hire while providing 24/7 processing capability, allowing you to invest in higher-level talent instead.

Key Takeaways

- **Start with the basics, scale strategically.** Begin with essential roles like a bookkeeper and add strategic expertise, such as a fractional CFO, as your business grows.

- **Use fractional expertise wisely.** Leverage part-time financial professionals until your business can justify full-time hires.

- **Let roles evolve with growth.** In the early stages, team members may wear multiple hats, but as transaction volume increases, specialization becomes necessary.

- **Know when to bring in specialists.** As your financial needs become more complex, ensure you have the right expertise to support accurate reporting and decision-making.

- **Cultivate relationships with external partners.** Work with financial advisors, tax professionals and lenders who can provide specialized insights when needed.

- **Tailor your finance team to your business model.** Your industry, growth stage and operational complexity should dictate how and when you expand your financial team.

AI Key Takeaway Addition

Consider AI before adding headcount. Automation tools can often handle routine accounting tasks more efficiently than additional staff, allowing you to invest in strategic rather than transactional resources.

With the right team in place, your next priority is putting safeguards around your financial processes to protect your business as it grows.

CHAPTER 3

Internal Controls & Processes

For small business CEOs, establishing robust internal controls might seem like overkill—something only necessary for large corporations with complex operations and regulatory requirements. In my years working with growing companies, I've witnessed firsthand how this misconception can lead to costly mistakes, fraud, operational inefficiencies and, in some cases, business failure.

The reality is that internal controls are not just bureaucratic red tape; they're vital guardians of your company's financial integrity. While a startup might be able to function with minimal controls, every growing business reaches a point where informal procedures no longer suffice. As your transaction volume increases and your team expands, the risk of errors, inefficiencies and even fraud grow exponentially.

Case Study:
The High Cost of Inadequate Controls

A promising technology services client with $4 million in revenue learned this lesson the hard way. Their office manager had complete control over accounts payable—entering vendor information, approving payments and reconciling bank statements. The CEO trusted her implicitly; she had been with the company since its founding.

Over 18 months, she embezzled nearly $180,000 by creating fictitious vendors and approving payments to accounts she controlled. The fraud was only discovered when she took an extended vacation, and a temporary replacement noticed discrepancies.

Beyond the direct financial loss, the company faced additional costs: forensic accounting services, legal fees, higher insurance premiums and, most painfully, damaged team morale and strained client relationships when the incident became known.

A simple segregation of duties policy—having separate people responsible for vendor setup and payment approval— would have prevented the entire situation.

In this chapter, I'll outline practical approaches to establishing essential internal controls that protect your business without creating unnecessary bureaucracy. These systems won't just reduce risk—they'll deliver measurable improvements to your operational efficiency, data reliability and decision-making capabilities.

Understanding Internal Controls

Internal controls are the processes, policies and procedures that safeguard your assets, ensure reliable financial reporting and promote operational efficiency. Think of them as your business's immune system—they prevent problems when possible and detect issues quickly when prevention fails.

Effective internal controls serve multiple purposes:

1. **Risk mitigation** – Reducing the probability and impact of negative events
2. **Fraud prevention and detection** – Creating barriers to dishonest behavior
3. **Efficiency improvement** – Streamlining operations through standardized processes
4. **Regulatory compliance** – Meeting legal and industry requirements
5. **Stakeholder confidence** – Building trust with investors, lenders and partners

While the concept might sound complex, the fundamental principle is straightforward: create a system of checks and balances where critical functions are distributed across multiple people or departments. This distribution ensures that no single individual has complete control over a transaction cycle—reducing both the risk and temptation for misconduct.

Accuracy & Completeness of Accounting Records

Accurate accounting records form the foundation of sound financial management. Without reliable data, even the most sophisticated analysis becomes meaningless—you'll be making critical decisions based on fiction rather than fact.

Key Control Mechanisms

Regular Reconciliations

Reconciliation—the process of comparing internal records against external sources—is your first line of defense against accounting errors. At a minimum, implement monthly reconciliations for your bank accounts, credit card statements, accounts receivable and payable aging reports and inventory records if applicable. The goal isn't simply to compare balances but to investigate any discrepancies until they're resolved. Even small differences can indicate systemic issues that could snowball over time if left unchecked.

Chart of Accounts Maintenance

A well-structured chart of accounts provides the organizational framework for your financial data, serving as the foundation for all financial reporting and analysis. Review it periodically to ensure it accurately reflects your current business model as your company evolves. We had a professional services client that "productized" a service offering and therefore, needed to add a new section of accounts to their chart of accounts to reflect the new business line.

Your account structure should facilitate meaningful financial analysis by grouping related items logically and at appropriate levels of detail.

We had another small subscription model business client that, when we started, had over 450 separate general ledger accounts. We rationalized the entire chart of accounts and reduced the number of individual accounts to under 100, thereby saving significant time to maintain their books and, more importantly, provide much more clarity for their financial reports.

Maintain consistent categorization across accounting periods to ensure comparability—random shifts in how similar expenses are coded make trend analysis impossible and can obscure important patterns. Additionally, design your account structure to support tax preparation needs by aligning with required reporting categories.

Most importantly, limit the ability to modify the chart of accounts to senior accounting staff, as improper changes can distort financial reporting and compromise the integrity of historical data.

Standardized Documentation

Establish clear requirements for supporting documentation across every type of financial transaction your business conducts. This means maintaining receipts for all expenses, signed contracts for services, approved purchase orders for significant purchases, formal invoices for all sales and detailed time records for billable services. This comprehensive documentation creates a robust audit trail that not only enables verification but provides valuable context for future reference, ensuring that knowledge about transactions doesn't walk out the door when employees leave.

For *a company with under \$5 million in revenue, this might look like:*

1. *Weekly review of cash receipts and disbursements by the CEO or designated manager*
2. *Monthly reconciliation of all bank and credit card accounts by your bookkeeper or accountant*
3. *Quarterly review of accounts receivable aging with follow-up on past-due accounts*
4. *Annual review of the chart of accounts with your external accountant*
5. *Cloud storage of all financial documentation with consistent naming conventions*

Prevention & Detection of Fraud and Errors

The Association of Certified Fraud Examiners estimates that businesses lose 5% of revenue to fraud annually, with small businesses facing disproportionately higher losses. While perfect prevention is impossible, well-designed controls significantly reduce your exposure.

Essential Fraud Prevention Controls

1. Segregation of Duties

The most fundamental fraud prevention control is separating key financial responsibilities among different employees. This means distributing critical functions—authorization, recording, custody and reconciliation—across multiple team members so that no single person controls an entire transaction from start to finish. Authorization involves approving transactions, while recording refers to documenting them in your accounting systems. Custody means handling physical assets or accessing credentials, and reconciliation involves verifying transaction accuracy. For example, the person who approves vendor payments should never be the same person who sets up vendor accounts in your system, as this creates an opportunity for fictitious vendor schemes.

2. Dual Control for Banking Activities

Banking activities represent your greatest point of vulnerability, as they provide direct access to your company's cash. Implement dual controls to mitigate this risk by requiring two signatures on checks above a defined threshold and separating the creation and approval of electronic payments. Additionally, limit bank account access to essential personnel and consider using positive pay services, which match checks presented for payment against those you've authorized, effectively preventing check tampering or forgery.

3. Independent Reviews

Regular independent reviews provide an additional layer of protection that can deter potential fraud and catch issues early. For example:

- Surprise audits of petty cash and other liquid assets create unpredictability that prevents fraudsters from hiding misappropriations. A manufacturing CEO implemented random weekly cash drawer counts that uncovered a pattern of "borrowing" by an otherwise trusted employee before the amounts escalated.
- Rotating duties, when possible, ensures no single person controls a process end-to-end for too long, reducing opportunities for concealment. One professional services firm rotated billing responsibilities quarterly, revealing inefficiencies and several billing errors that had gone unnoticed for months.
- Management review of unusual transactions—particularly those just below approval thresholds or occurring at odd times—often reveals red flags. A retail business owner who began personally reviewing all refunds over $200 identified a cashier processing fraudulent returns to friends.
- Periodic third-party assessments bring fresh eyes to your processes, as an automotive repair shop discovered when an external review identified a parts ordering scheme that internal controls had missed due to familiarity blindness.

4. System Access Controls

Your financial software contains the keys to your kingdom, making technological controls absolutely essential. Implement role-based system access that limits users to only the functions they need to perform their jobs. Enforce regular password changes and promptly terminate system access when employees leave the company. Maintain comprehensive audit logs that track who made changes to critical data and when those changes occurred, creating a digital paper trail that deters inappropriate actions and helps investigate any irregularities.

In a small company with few employees, perfect segregation of duties may be impossible. Alternative controls for small teams include:

- Owner/CEO review of bank statements and reconciliations
- Use of technology solutions that enforce approval workflows
- Periodic reviews by your external accountant or fractional CFO
- Employee rotation for key tasks when possible
- Mandatory vacation policies (fraud is often discovered when the perpetrator is away)

Safeguarding of Assets

Your business assets, whether physical, financial or intellectual, represent significant investments that require protection against theft, misuse and obsolescence.

Physical Asset Controls

Inventory Management

For product-based businesses, inventory often represents a significant portion of assets and presents unique control challenges. Conduct regular physical inventory counts to verify that your records match reality and restrict warehouse access to authorized personnel to prevent unauthorized removal of goods.

Every inventory movement should be documented with appropriate approvals, creating a chain of accountability. When discrepancies inevitably arise, investigate them promptly. Patterns in these discrepancies often point to process failures or potentially fraudulent activities that require attention.

Fixed Asset Protection

Equipment, vehicles and other fixed assets represent substantial investments that demand thoughtful protection strategies. Maintain a detailed fixed asset register that includes serial numbers, purchase dates, costs, and current locations. For physical items, consider tagging assets with identifiers where appropriate, making ownership clear and theft more difficult.

When your business owns mobile equipment that moves between locations or employees, implement formal check-out procedures to track responsibility. Finally, perform periodic physical verification to ensure these valuable assets haven't disappeared through theft or been forgotten during business operations.

Cash Management

Cash remains one of your most vulnerable assets, demanding particularly stringent controls. Minimizing cash on hand by encouraging electronic payments dramatically reduces your risk profile. For example, a restaurant owner shifted to a primarily card-based system, keeping only minimal cash for emergency transactions, which eliminated three instances of theft they had experienced in the previous year. For the cash you must maintain, invest in a quality safe with strictly limited access—ideally restricted to just one or two trusted individuals with separate access codes that create an audit trail of who opened it and when.

Daily cash deposits are essential, even when amounts seem small. A retail business that implemented mandatory end-of-day deposits discovered this not only reduced theft risk but improved their cash flow forecasting accuracy by keeping bank balances current. Every cash transaction, no matter how minor, should be documented through point-of-sale systems or manual logs. For instance, one construction company CEO implemented a simple carbon-copy receipt book for field payments and uncovered a pattern of missing funds that had been occurring for months but was disguised by inconsistent record-keeping.

Remember, cash controls protect honest employees as much as they deter dishonest ones—clear procedures eliminate ambiguity about handling practices and remove opportunities for suspicion when discrepancies occur.

Tip: Not every company handles physical cash, but as a CEO, you need to ensure that your bank accounts are properly protected. For all our B2B clients, we recommend a stringent process for creating new vendors in the clients' accounting platforms. The vendor's bank information must be **verbally** verified with a known representative from the vendor's staff. Do not take for granted that the bank account and routing numbers on the first invoice you receive are indeed correct!

Intellectual Property Controls

For many businesses, intellectual property represents their most valuable asset, often exceeding the worth of physical property by orders of magnitude. Protecting these intangible assets begins with comprehensive confidentiality agreements for everyone who touches your business—from full-time employees to temporary contractors and vendors. A software company I worked with discovered a competitor had launched a similar product because their contractor agreements lacked specific non-disclosure provisions.

Beyond legal protections, implement technological safeguards with role-based access controls that limit sensitive information to only those who genuinely need it. Establishing clear ownership of work product in all contracts prevents costly disputes; one marketing agency CEO found himself unable to use content his company had paid to develop because their agreement didn't explicitly transfer copyright ownership.

Finally, don't overlook formal protections—registering trademarks, patents, and copyrights provides significant legal advantages if infringement occurs, as a consumer products company discovered when they successfully defended their distinctive packaging design only because they had registered years earlier.

Policies & Procedures to Ensure Orderly Operations

Documented policies and procedures create consistency, enhance efficiency and reduce dependence on specific individuals. They transform tribal knowledge into organizational knowledge, which is a critical step in building a scalable business.

Essential Financial Policies

Accounting Policies Manual

A comprehensive accounting policies manual serves as the financial constitution of your organization, documenting the principles that govern your financial reporting. This document should clearly articulate your revenue recognition criteria—when you consider a sale complete and recordable—along with expense categorization guidelines that ensure consistent classification. Include your asset capitalization thresholds that distinguish between expenses and capital investments, as well as your chosen depreciation and amortization methods. Don't forget to document your month-end closing procedures to ensure consistency in your financial reporting cycles, especially as you experience employee turnover.

Procurement Policies

Well-crafted procurement policies protect your company from overspending, conflicts of interest and vendor dependency risks. Establish clear authorization levels that delineate who can approve expenditures at different dollar thresholds—perhaps allowing managers to approve routine expenses up to $1,000 while requiring executive approval for larger purchases.

For significant expenditures, implement competitive bidding requirements that ensure you're getting fair market value. Require conflict of interest disclosures from employees involved in purchasing decisions and document your vendor selection criteria to promote objectivity. Finally, establish guidelines for payment terms management that balance cash flow considerations with vendor relationships.

Expense Reimbursement Policies

Create clear guidelines for employee expenses that eliminate ambiguity and set consistent expectations across your organization. Here are some everyday issues to address:

- **Define eligible expense categories** so employees know in advance whether client entertainment, professional development, or home office supplies qualify for reimbursement. A technology CEO found that clearly distinguishing between reimbursable business travel and non-reimbursable commuting expenses reduced disputes by over 80%.
- Establish specific **documentation requirements**—such as itemized receipts rather than just credit card slips—to ensure proper substantiation for both accounting and tax purposes.
- Implement reasonable **submission deadlines** that balance employee cash flow needs with your accounting cycle. One manufacturing company moved from monthly to bi-weekly expense processing after discovering employees were delaying major purchases to avoid out-of-pocket costs.
- Design a straightforward **approval workflow** that routes expenses to the appropriate manager while maintaining separation of duties.
- Finally, communicate **clear expectations about payment timing** so employees know when reimbursements will arrive in their accounts. A professional services firm that committed to processing approved expenses within five business days saw dramatic improvements in policy compliance and employee satisfaction.

Revenue Management Policies

Document comprehensive processes for revenue management that protect both your top line and cash flow. For instance:

- Establish structured customer credit approval procedures that evaluate creditworthiness consistently rather than making ad hoc decisions. One wholesale distributor implemented a tiered credit matrix that reduced bad debt by 40% while still accommodating valuable customers with appropriate limits.

- Clearly define pricing authority by specifying who can offer discounts and their maximum thresholds—a software company CEO discovered unauthorized discounting was eroding margins by 6% until they implemented approval requirements for reductions exceeding 10%.
- Set consistent rules for invoice generation timing to ensure prompt billing. A consulting firm that shifted from monthly to weekly invoicing dramatically improved its cash conversion cycle.
- Develop standardized collection procedures that escalate appropriately from friendly reminders to formal demand letters, with clear triggers for each step.
- Finally, establish protocols for handling bad debt, including when to involve collection agencies, when to consider write-offs, and how to document these decisions for both accounting and tax purposes. A manufacturing company implemented quarterly bad debt reviews with formalized documentation requirements that not only improved their financial reporting but also helped identify problematic customer segments that warranted tighter credit controls.

Tip: Policy documentation should be proportional to your company's size and complexity. For small businesses, focus on documenting the most critical procedures first. Those that: involve significant financial impact, require coordination across multiple people, are performed infrequently and would be difficult to reconstruct if the primary person were unavailable.

A five-page document covering critical processes is more valuable than a hundred-page manual that no one reads.

Timely Preparation of Reliable Financial Information

Accurate financial information delivered promptly enables better decision-making and helps identify issues before they become crises. The most sophisticated controls are worthless if they delay financial reporting to the point where the information loses its relevance.

Financial Reporting Controls

Standardized Month-End Close Process

A consistent closing process is the foundation of reliable financial reporting. This means developing a detailed closing checklist that clearly outlines each required task, who's responsible for it, and when it must be completed. For example, your accounting manager might be responsible for reconciling all bank accounts by the third business day of each month, while your controller reviews all journal entries by the fifth day. Each step should have built-in review procedures before finalization to catch errors early. Many small businesses find that moving from an ad-hoc approach to a standardized process can reduce their closing time from weeks to just a few days.

Management Review Controls

Beyond the basic accounting procedures, effective management review is critical. This means regularly comparing your current results against both your budget projections and prior period performance. When your gross margin suddenly drops by 5% compared to last month, this review process ensures you'll notice it immediately rather than discovering it when it's too late to address the underlying cause. Each review should include formal sign-off by the appropriate personnel, whether that's your CFO or, in smaller organizations, yourself as the CEO. Any significant judgments or estimates, such as inventory obsolescence calculations or bad debt reserves, should be documented with clear rationales that can stand up to scrutiny.

Financial Systems Integration

Manual data entry is the enemy of both speed and accuracy. Integrating your financial systems can dramatically reduce errors while accelerating your reporting timeline. If your point-of-sale system automatically feeds data to your accounting software each night, you'll eliminate hours of manual entry and the inevitable errors that come with it.

Each integration should include validation checks to ensure data integrity—for instance, confirming that sales totals match between systems. Maintain comprehensive audit trails for all automated processes and periodically test these integrations to verify they're functioning as expected. One small manufacturing CEO discovered that a previously undetected integration error had been consistently understating cost of goods sold by 3% for months, significantly affecting pricing decisions.

Financial Calendar

A well-structured financial calendar serves as your roadmap throughout the year. This calendar should clearly mark the following:

- Monthly close deadlines
- When reports will be distributed to stakeholders
- Key tax filing deadlines
- Budget development timelines
- External audit schedules.

Having this calendar visible to all finance team members creates accountability and helps everyone plan their work accordingly. For example, knowing that bank covenant reporting is due by the 15th of each month means your team understands why the monthly close must be completed by the 10th. This forward-looking approach prevents the fire drills that occur when deadlines are suddenly remembered at the last minute.

Technology's Role in Internal Controls

Technology's Role in Internal Controls

While internal controls have traditionally been process-focused, technology now plays a central role in their implementation. Modern accounting and business systems incorporate many controls directly into their workflows, often making them more effective and less burdensome to maintain.

Key Technology Solutions

Accounting Software

Your choice of accounting software forms the backbone of your financial control environment. Modern solutions offer sophisticated protections that manual systems simply cannot match. For instance, role-based access controls ensure your sales team can enter orders but cannot approve credit limits, while your accounting staff can process payments but cannot create new vendors.

These systems maintain comprehensive audit trails that record who did what and when, creating accountability throughout the organization. For instance, a small retail business owner I worked with discovered an unusual pattern of after-hours inventory adjustments through audit trail reports, ultimately uncovering employee theft that had gone unnoticed for months. Look for software that includes automated reconciliation capabilities to flag discrepancies immediately rather than discovering them weeks later during manual reviews.

Expense Management Systems

Digital expense management transforms what was once a paper-heavy, delay-prone process into a streamlined control point. When employees can simply photograph receipts with their smartphones at the point of purchase, compliance improves dramatically. These systems enforce policy at the submission stage—alerting employees when they've exceeded meal allowances or selected an unauthorized expense category—rather than creating awkward conversations after the fact. Automated approval routing ensures the right manager reviews each expense without the delays of routing physical documents. One technology CEO found that implementing digital expense management reduced processing costs by 75% while improving compliance with travel policies. The direct integration with accounting systems eliminates duplicate entries and ensures expenses hit the right accounts consistently.

Banking Technology

Modern banking platforms offer powerful controls that weren't available even a decade ago. Positive pay systems allow you to pre-authorize checks before they clear, preventing unauthorized payments. Multi-factor authentication ensures that even if passwords are compromised, unauthorized users can't access your accounts. Segregated user roles might allow your bookkeeper to initiate payments while requiring CFO approval before funds move. Real-time transaction alerts notify you immediately of unusual activity, such as large withdrawals or international transfers. A construction company owner I advised received an alert about an unexpected $40,000 wire transfer request, enabling him to block what turned out to be a sophisticated fraud attempt before any money left the account.

Document Management

Digital document management transforms how you store and access critical business records. Rather than searching through filing cabinets for last year's insurance policy, structured filing systems allow instant retrieval of any document. Version control ensures you're always working with the current contract rather than an outdated draft. Access restrictions prevent sensitive information like employee records or intellectual property from being viewed by unauthorized personnel. Proper retention policies automatically archive or destroy documents according to legal requirements, reducing both storage costs and legal risk. A healthcare services CEO implemented digital document management and discovered that what once required a full-time records clerk now happens automatically while also improving their audit readiness and reducing preparation time by weeks.

__Tip__: Don't get seduced by cutting-edge technology if you haven't mastered the basics. A $50,000 ERP system won't fix fundamental control weaknesses. Start with improving your core processes, then add technology that enhances those processes.

Building a Control Environment That Works

The most carefully designed controls will fail without a supportive organizational culture. Internal controls aren't just about rules and procedures; they're about creating an environment where ethical behavior is expected and valued.

Establishing a Strong Control Environment

Tone at the Top

As CEO, your attitude toward controls fundamentally shapes your organization's approach to compliance and ethics. When you consistently follow the same protocols you expect from your team—whether it's submitting expense reports on time or adhering to approval limits—you send a powerful message about your company's values.

One manufacturing CEO I worked with made a point of having his expense reports reviewed by his CFO in the same manner as every other employee, despite technically having the authority to approve his own expenses. This simple act communicated volumes about accountability. Regularly discussing controls in team meetings helps underscore their importance, while publicly recognizing employees who identify control weaknesses or demonstrate exceptional ethical judgment reinforces desired behaviors.

When control failures occur, addressing them promptly and consistently—regardless of who was involved—demonstrates that no one is above the rules.

Clear Expectations

Employees can't follow procedures they don't understand or don't know exist. Effective control environments begin with clear job descriptions that specifically include control responsibilities. For example, a purchasing manager's job description should explicitly state their role in vendor verification and payment authorization. New employee onboarding should cover key control procedures relevant to their position, not as an afterthought but as a core component of their role. For instance, a software company CEO implemented quarterly "control refreshers" that focused on different aspects of their control environment, which dramatically reduced policy exceptions. All policies should be easily accessible in a central location, written in plain language that focuses on the "why" behind requirements, not just the "what."

Open Communication

Controls are strengthened when employees feel empowered to raise concerns without fear. Creating multiple reporting channels—direct supervisors, HR, anonymous hotlines—ensures that issues can be raised even when one path might be compromised. One retail business owner established a simple anonymous suggestion box and discovered inventory control weaknesses that employees had noticed but were hesitant to mention directly.

Whistleblower protections must be more than just words in a policy; they require active protection from retaliation. When control issues are identified, transparent communication about what happened and what's changing helps build trust. For example, a healthcare CEO turned a significant billing error into a learning opportunity by openly discussing how it occurred and the new procedures implemented to prevent recurrence rather than hiding the incident.

Regular Assessment

A static control environment quickly becomes outdated and ineffective. Periodic risk assessments should examine where your business has evolved and what new vulnerabilities might exist. Has your expansion into ecommerce created payment processing risks that weren't present when you only sold through physical locations? Regular testing of key controls—from surprise cash counts to simulated phishing attempts—helps identify weaknesses before they're exploited.

A construction company instituted quarterly "control drills" where they tested employee responses to common fraud scenarios, significantly improving their team's ability to recognize red flags. Every near-miss and actual incident should be treated as a learning opportunity, with formal reviews to identify what worked, what didn't, and what needs to change going forward.

Implementing Controls in a Growing Business

Implementing controls is not an all-or-nothing proposition. A phased approach based on your company's size, resources and risk profile will yield the best results without overwhelming your team.

Implementation Roadmap

For Startups (Under $1M Revenue)

Focus on fundamental protections:

- Basic segregation of financial duties (even with limited staff)
- CEO review of all bank statements
- Documented approval process for all expenditures
- Secure storage of financial records
- Regular reconciliation of bank accounts

For Growing Businesses ($1 million to $5 million in Revenue)

Add more structured controls:

- Formal accounting policies
- Defined approval matrices for spending
- Regular financial review meetings
- Basic IT security protocols
- External accountant reviews of quarterly financials

For Established Businesses ($5 million to $25 million in Revenue)

Implement comprehensive systems:

- Detailed policy and procedure documentation
- Automated workflow approvals
- Regular internal control audits
- Dedicated finance leadership (Controller or CFO)
- Advanced system security and access controls

For Scaling Businesses ($25 million+ in Revenue)

Add sophisticated oversight:

- Internal audit function
- Audit committee oversight
- Enterprise risk management program
- Compliance monitoring systems
- Comprehensive control testing

AI Tip

Implement AI-powered fraud detection that monitors transaction patterns and flags unusual activities automatically. Unlike manual controls that depend on human oversight, AI never sleeps and can identify suspicious patterns across thousands of transactions that would be impossible to catch manually.

Key Takeaways

- Internal controls are essential at every stage of business growth. They safeguard finances, prevent fraud and ensure operational efficiency.

- Segregation of duties strengthens financial oversight. Dividing responsibilities reduces errors and prevents misuse of company assets.

- Documented policies turn personal knowledge into company-wide standards. A well-defined framework minimizes risks tied to key personnel turnover.

- Technology should support, not replace, sound financial controls. Automated workflows enhance security but must be paired with strong processes.

- Leadership sets the tone for a strong control environment. Clear communication and a commitment to ethical standards create accountability.

- Start with high-risk areas and expand gradually. A phased approach ensures controls grow with the business without overwhelming operations.

- Continuous review and adaptation keep controls effective. Regular assessments prevent gaps as your business scales and evolves.

AI Key Takeaway Addition:

Strengthen controls with AI monitoring. AI-powered fraud detection and transaction monitoring provide continuous oversight that enhances traditional internal controls without adding administrative burden.

As the ancient saying goes, "The best time to plant a tree was twenty years ago. The second-best time is now." The same applies to implementing internal controls. Because solid internal controls create discipline.

But without the right tools and technology, even the best team can struggle. Let's look at how your tech stack can streamline and strengthen your finance function.

CHAPTER 4

Technology for Finance & Accounting

N othing is more frustrating than outdated technology that creates more problems than it solves. Yet it's common for a company's needs to change as it grows and for systems to become obsolete. Therefore, you must stay on top of what is and is not creating efficiencies, or the technology that was once so helpful can become a big nuisance.

For example, early-stage companies often acquire disparate solutions for payment processing, expense reimbursement, time sheet management and billing. That is normal. But while discrete solutions can initially be more efficient and cost effective than an all-in-one accounting solution, they won't work forever.

So, how do you know when you have outgrown your accounting tech? Here are some clues:

- You must export data from your current solution into Excel for manipulation before producing the financial reports you need for decision-making.
- You must reenter the same information in more than one system.
- Instead of paying your employees and vendors directly through the bank, you still print and mail physical checks.
- Your current system does not have a built-in payment approval queue—a feature that is unnecessary when a company is small but essential for those paying 25+ vendors.

Implementing financial software for small businesses is a crucial step in improving the efficiency and accuracy of financial management processes. It is important for CEOs to understand the benefits of utilizing financial software to streamline accounting, budgeting and reporting tasks. By implementing the right financial software, you can save time, reduce errors and gain valuable insight into your company's financial health.

One of the key benefits of implementing financial software for small businesses is the automation of repetitive tasks. With financial software, you can automate tasks such as invoicing, payroll processing and financial reporting, saving you valuable time and reducing the risk of human error. This automation allows you to focus on more strategic tasks that drive your business forward, rather than getting bogged down in manual data entry and calculations.

In addition to automation, financial software also provides real-time access to financial data, allowing you to make informed decisions based on up-to-date information. By having a clear view of your company's financial performance, you can identify trends, monitor cash flow and make adjustments to your budget and business strategy as needed. This real-time access to data is essential for small businesses looking to stay agile and responsive in today's fast-paced business environment.

Furthermore, financial software can help small businesses improve their financial forecasting and planning processes. By using advanced forecasting tools and scenario analysis capabilities, you can better predict future financial outcomes and plan for various business scenarios.

This proactive approach to financial planning can help you anticipate challenges, seize opportunities and make strategic decisions that drive growth and profitability.

Overall, implementing financial software for small businesses is a smart investment that can help you streamline financial processes, improve decision-making and drive business growth. By leveraging financial software, you can take control of your company's finances, reduce risks and position your business for long-term success. As a CEO of a small business, it is essential to embrace technology and prioritize financial software implementation to stay competitive.

Leveraging Technology for Financial Efficiency

In today's rapidly evolving business landscape, leveraging technology is essential for small businesses to achieve financial efficiency. As the CEO of a small business, it is crucial to understand how technology can streamline financial processes and improve overall profitability. By embracing the latest tools and systems, you can gain a competitive edge and position your company for long-term success.

One key way to leverage technology for financial efficiency is through the implementation of cloud-based accounting software. These platforms allow you to centralize your financial data, automate repetitive tasks and generate real-time reports. When you have access to up-to-date financial information, you can make informed decisions quickly and effectively. Additionally, cloud-based accounting software can help reduce human error and improve the accuracy of your financial records.

Another way to harness technology for financial efficiency is by utilizing digital payment solutions. From online invoicing to electronic payment processing, these tools can streamline your accounts receivable and accounts payable processes. By offering customers multiple payment options and automating payment reminders, you can improve cash flow and reduce late payments. Digital payment solutions also provide added security and convenience for both you and your customers.

Furthermore, leveraging technology for financial efficiency can involve implementing data analytics tools to gain valuable insights into your company's financial performance. By analyzing key metrics and trends, you can identify areas for improvement, optimize your budgeting and forecasting processes and make data-driven decisions. Data analytics can also help you track the success of your financial strategies and adjust them as needed to achieve your business goals.

Real World Example

In 2024, my firm, The CEO's Right Hand implemented a complete overhaul of our firm's technology solution set (a.k.a. our "tech stack.") We had followed the same exact playbook of millions of other small businesses and had cobbled together a variety of non-integrated, spot solutions for our finance and accounting applications.

While each application satisfied the individual requirements of that piece of the puzzle, when it came to trying to get data from one to the other, or consolidated reporting, it became unwieldly and error prone. We had a myriad of different applications: CRM (Zoho CRM), accounting (QuickBooks), Invoicing (FreshBooks), Timesheet Tracking (FreshBooks), Customer Payments (Stripe), Contracts (Tango Agreements), Chase (Vendor Payments) and even Excel (Contractor Payouts).

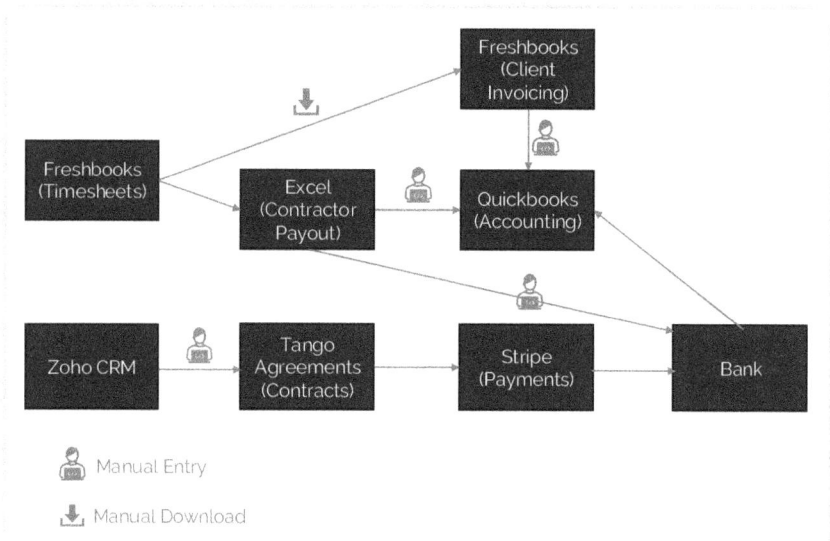

TCRH's Tech Stack (Before)

As the company was entering the "scale" phase of our evolution, we needed a better solution. We needed integrated ERP (Enterprise Resource Planning) software that would act as a centralized platform to manage all aspects of our financial operations. This included recording transactions, managing accounts payable and receivable, generating contracts, tracking time and project profitability—essentially integrating accounting functions with other business processes like sales, delivery and human resources within a single system.

Since we were already users of the Zoho platform, I saw that they provided several other applications (modules) that would potentially meet our needs. I met with a certified Zoho partner and showed them how we were currently operating, and they provided me with a demo of the Zoho platform which made it abundantly clear that we were doing it the hard way.

It took several months to get the system up and running and configured to meet our needs, but we now have a fully integrated solution that spans every aspect of the finance and accounting function, except for financial planning, which we still do in Excel. We have integrated every aspect of the "order-to-cash" flow: initial contract, tracking consultant time/project delivery, billing the clients, paying the contractors, accounts receivable collection, client payments and booking the cash upon receipt. Clients have access to their invoices and payments via a "customer portal" and contractors have similar access to their own portal.

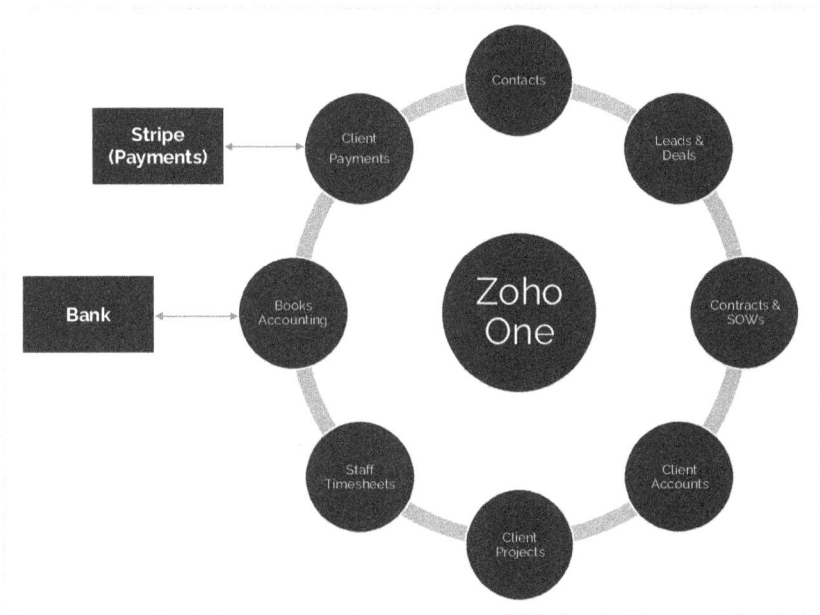

TCRH's Current Integrated Tech Stack

As a CEO of a small business, it is essential to embrace technology as a powerful tool for improving financial efficiency. By investing in cloud-based accounting software, digital payment solutions and data analytics tools, you can streamline your financial processes, enhance decision-making and drive overall profitability. By staying informed about the latest technological advancements in financial management, you can position your company for sustainable growth and success in today's competitive business environment.

AI Tip

When evaluating new financial technology, prioritize solutions with built-in AI capabilities rather than standalone systems. AI-enhanced accounting platforms can automatically categorize expenses, predict cash flow, and generate insights from your data, providing more value than traditional software that simply stores information.

Key Takeaways

- **Upgrade technology before inefficiencies cost you.** Outdated or disconnected financial tools slow operations, introduce errors and limit business growth. Regularly assess whether your current systems still meet your needs.

- **Automation improves accuracy and saves time.** Cloud-based accounting software and digital payment solutions reduce manual work, minimize errors and provide real-time financial insights.

- **Integrated systems enhance efficiency.** A centralized financial tech stack eliminates redundant data entry, improves reporting and streamlines financial processes like invoicing, payments and expense tracking.

- **Use data analytics to drive better financial decisions.** Leveraging financial metrics and real-time reporting allows CEOs to identify trends, optimize cash flow and adjust strategies proactively.

- **Technology is a competitive advantage.** The right financial tools enable small businesses to scale efficiently, improve financial forecasting and make informed, data-driven decisions that support long-term success.

AI Key Takeaway Addition

Choose AI-enhanced technology platforms. Modern financial systems with built-in AI capabilities provide automated insights and predictions that traditional software cannot match.

With your team and systems aligned, you're ready to shift focus to the future. That starts with building a solid financial plan and forecast.

PART 2

Planning, Monitoring & Managing Performance

CHAPTER 5

Financial Planning & Forecasting

When I talk to CEOs and founders, financial planning, specifically budgeting and forecasting, is often one of their biggest challenges. Many struggle with how to build and use a financial model, finding it complex or overwhelming.

The real challenge? Translating all the moving parts of a business (some of which are hard to quantify) into a clear, actionable financial plan. For some, just the thought of structuring it into a spreadsheet feels daunting.

The worst-case scenario? A CEO who doesn't even realize why a forecast is essential. Without a forecast, you're flying blind, making decisions based on gut feelings rather than data. So, let's start by understanding why forecasting matters and how to simplify the process.

Why Plan?

Forecasting may not be a top-of-the-list item on the minds of entrepreneurs and small business owners. But failing to take a forward-looking, bird's-eye view of a business could lead to critical mistakes and a lack of direction. This situation could be avoided with a well-devised, objective forecast based on sound data.

Forecasting, when done right, is more than a simple prediction. A business forecast is based on a deep analysis of information about the company, the industry and the economy. It becomes a critical resource that management can use to prepare for and get ahead of market changes. And it allows you to establish realistic plans for the future of your business instead of just winging it.

Using a financial plan is like using any other tool in your toolkit to help grow and scale a business. Just like a CRM is used to manage your sales pipeline, a financial model is used to help you make informed decisions about the business.

Tip: One of the most frequent "pain points" I hear from prospective clients is the following: "I don't know if I can afford [fill in the blank]." CEOs who do not have a proper forecasting function, including cashflow planning, are indeed flying blind and cannot make timely or effective decisions about their business.

Strategic Planning

Each year, most companies go through what is called "budget time." We've all heard the proverbial: "I can't make a decision until after we do the budget!" *But what exactly is meant by budget time?*

The lion's share of companies think budgeting refers to an Excel model built 10 years ago containing an income statement forecast, repurposed year after year. Executive management will simply take last year's numbers and increase or decrease them by certain percentages (and the sales budget will almost always increase). The budget is done! Now onto running the business like we did last year...

Unfortunately, budgets often end up shelved in some server directory or thrown in a desk drawer. Worse yet, many budgets aren't completed until months into the new fiscal year. If the budget IS used, it's rarely compared with actual results, which is the main reason to budget in the first place. Thus, the entire effort oftentimes adds little to no value and takes precious time and energy away from running the day-to-day business.

For budget time to make any sense, it must include an element of strategic thinking. Enter strategic planning. Without strategic planning, Lewis Carroll's famous refrain from *Alice in Wonderland* applies to the business: "If you don't know where you're going, any road will take you there." Strategic planning precedes the budget and is the qualitative roadmap to reaching next year's financial goals. It follows then that the budget is the strategic plan expressed in quantitative terms. Both must be bound together to add any real value to the other and to serve as a guide for executive management's execution of business operations.

For a small business CEO, the strategic planning process can be simplified but should not be ignored. Take the time to stop working "in" the business for a day or two. Meet with your management team or outside advisors to review the high-level goals for the company and your progress. Understand what needs to change, if anything, to achieve your goals for the coming 3–5 years. Then, translate that back into what must happen in the coming 12 months that "moves the ball down the field" (i.e. provides you with the necessary wins towards the ultimate goal, whatever that goal may be).

Budget vs. Plan vs. Forecast

Many CEOs confuse the terms budget, plan and forecast, so let's break them down clearly.

- **Budget (a.k.a. the Annual 'Plan'):** A budget is created once a year and serves as a financial roadmap for the upcoming year, outlining expected revenues and expenses. Larger companies may also budget for assets like cash, inventory and equipment. More sophisticated businesses involve multiple departments in the process, using past performance to create a comprehensive plan. Smaller businesses may lack the resources to conduct such a detailed process, but that doesn't mean they should skip budgeting altogether—it's a critical part of financial management.
- **Forecast:** A forecast is an ongoing update to the budget that reflects new information as the year progresses. Unlike a budget, which is fixed at the start of the year, a forecast adjusts based on actual performance and evolving business conditions—such as changes in sales, costs or market trends.

For CEOs who want a clear picture of where their business is heading, a forecast should be updated at least quarterly, if not monthly. This allows for quicker decision-making and helps businesses stay responsive to market changes.

Ways Forecasting Fails

It is possible to make a bad forecast. By definition, forecasting is a way of looking into the future, and it is unlikely to be 100% accurate. However, one can conduct forecasts with greater confidence if potential shortcomings are identified in advance and kept in check.

Some common causes of poor forecasting include the following:

Not taking it seriously

Companies that believe a budgeting exercise is sufficient could fall into this trap. Management or the finance team may only conduct forecasts occasionally or reactively. This could lead to inaccuracies and almost always defeats the point of forecasting, which is to equip the business for the future. Forecasts that are taken lightly and not fully understood may not have the credibility needed in the planning stages that follow.

Ignoring reality

Planning done around pipe dreams rather than real circumstances may lead to less-than-effective forecasts. Aspirational goals are necessary for running a business, but forecasts should be based on facts and verifiable data. That will then serve as the basis for realistic changes and growth that management can digest.

Using bad data

A forecast is only as sound as the data on which it is based. Accurate quantitative predictions cannot be made if the underlying data points are insufficient or built on faulty assumptions. A mistake in a calculation somewhere in the process could have an outsized effect on the output and great consequences if left unchecked.

Incorporating biases

Individuals have different ways of viewing the world, and this is sometimes based on biases. An entrepreneur may be overly optimistic, or a management team too conservative. Some may be driven by confirmation bias and search for or interpret data in ways that confirm their pre-existing beliefs or conclusions. For this reason, guidelines and various levels of checks should be in place to ensure that analyses are conducted in an objective manner.

Forecasting Best Practices

Forecasting is not an exact science, and there is no single right way to do it. Nevertheless, it is a key aspect in managing a business for the future. When combined with detailed budgets and open communication among departments and leadership, a forecast can be an essential tool with which to navigate a business toward success. Here are some suggestions for improving your financial forecasting:

Develop a process

Many companies have now adopted a quarterly rolling forecasting process instead of the traditional annual cycle. A rolling forecast requires the timely collection of business data and key inputs that will drive the forecast model. So, it is important that the company develops a robust process to drive collaboration between the business analytics function, the forecasting function and key stakeholders so it can incorporate business insights and decisions into the forecast.

Understand your business drivers

Good forecasting cannot exist without a firm grasp of the underlying business drivers, which translate into the inputs feeding the forecast model. At a minimum, the forecasting team should have a clear understanding of the key factors impacting their revenue and variable costs, such as pricing, volume drivers and product distribution channels.

Keep it simple

There are many forecasting methods, and it might take time for each company to determine the best approach for its business and industry. In general, there is no need to use overly complicated techniques in financial forecasting when simple methods (such as moving average) might be effective.

Samples

The following is a sample forecast that we put together for a professional services client using a straightforward template in Excel:

	Jan-24 Jan	Feb-24 Feb	Mar-24 Mar	Apr-24 Apr	May-24 May	Jun-24 Jun	Jul-24 Jul	Aug-24 Aug	Sep-24 Sep
REVENUES									
New Clients									
Existing Clients	345,532	377,151	380,220	385,040	429,801	454,440	427,701	452,016	358,147
TOTAL REVENUES	345,532	377,151	380,220	385,040	429,801	454,440	427,701	452,016	358,147
Total Cost of Revenues	226,934	231,599	262,681	255,364	274,742	243,537	261,484	253,864	233,049
GROSS PROFIT	118,598	145,552	117,539	129,676	155,060	210,903	166,217	198,152	125,098
Gross Profit Margin	34.3%	38.6%	30.9%	33.7%	36.1%	46.4%	38.9%	43.8%	34.9%
OPERATING EXPENSES									
General & Admin	17,878	17,755	27,628	34,864	39,467	32,177	40,619	41,619	44,802
Customer Support	11,667	14,417	18,207	21,140	15,392	14,805	15,802	15,017	19,098
Marketing	18,391	20,048	19,241	20,161	20,081	19,812	20,020	20,080	23,828
Sales	25,040	24,991	29,405	28,517	28,021	30,759	31,503	32,568	1,991
Staff Success									
Bonus Pool	3,459	3,530	3,836	3,865	4,328	4,489	4,299	4,501	3,703
TOTAL OPERATING EXPENSES	76,434	80,741	98,317	108,546	107,289	102,042	112,242	113,785	93,422
OPERATING INCOME	42,164	64,811	19,223	21,129	47,771	108,861	53,975	84,367	31,676
Operating Margin	12.2%	17.2%	5.1%	5.5%	11.1%	24.0%	12.6%	18.7%	8.8%

Each line item in the forecast, e.g., "Revenues, New Clients" has a detailed subsection containing the assumptions and formulas needed to create the total you see above.

For our smaller clients, we built a solution we call Right Hand Reports™, which includes a budgeting module so that we can quickly create budgets/forecasts for early-stage growth companies that do not have the same complexities as larger firms. The following shows the budget for a comparable size and type of business using Right Hand Reports:

Forecast

Profit & Loss   Balance Sheet   Cash Flow   Drivers

	2024						
Financial Services	281,363	294,969	293,425	298,801	325,771	344,739	357,075
Human Resources	48,396	65,759	55,393	48,949	68,002	61,628	61,832
Other Revenues	8,125	11,844	26,750	32,488	32,356	32,479	33,066
Recurring Accounting	8,000	8,000	8,000	8,000	8,000	8,240	8,487
Total Revenue	**345,885**	**353,002**	**383,568**	**386,767**	**434,129**	**447,086**	**460,460**
Cost of Goods Sold							
Cost of Goods Sold	0	173	0	637	841	493	657
Cost of Revenues	231,423	226,937	263,109	258,100	271,068	264,994	265,233
Total Cost of Goods Sold	231,423	227,110	263,109	258,737	271,909	265,486	265,890
Gross Profit Before Depreciation	114,461	125,892	120,459	128,029	162,219	181,600	194,571
Expenses							
Client Success	11,667	14,417	18,207	21,140	15,392	18,671	18,626
General & Administrative E...	17,946	16,604	27,078	31,858	37,764	37,608	38,730
JPP Bonus Expense	5,188	5,316	5,692	5,802	6,499	5,998	6,099
Marketing	18,391	20,043	19,241	20,161	20,061	21,868	23,658
Cash on Hand	$95,824	$81,377	$81,395	$119,688	$73,181	$179,273	$291,817

AI Tip

Replace static annual budgets with AI-driven dynamic forecasting that updates predictions based on real-time data and market conditions. AI can incorporate external factors like seasonal trends, economic indicators, and industry benchmarks to provide more accurate projections than spreadsheet-based models.

Key Takeaways

- **Set an annual budget and track progress.** Regularly compare actual results to your budget to stay on course, identify trends and make data-driven decisions.

- **Use forecasts to stay agile.** Update assumptions throughout the year to adjust for market changes, unexpected costs and new revenue opportunities.

- **Ensure accuracy with a structured process.** A disciplined approach to budgeting and forecasting improves reliability and helps avoid costly financial missteps.

- **Align your leadership team.** Engaging key stakeholders in the budgeting and forecasting process fosters alignment, accountability and commitment to company goals.

AI Key Takeaway Addition

Enhance forecasting with AI algorithms. AI-powered forecasting provides more accurate predictions by analyzing patterns and external factors that traditional models miss.

Even the best plan can fall apart without cash. Next, we'll cover how to manage cash flow so your business can survive, and you can achieve the outcomes you desire.

CHAPTER 6

Cash Flow Management

N early every business leader experiences a cash flow problem at some point. And it doesn't matter if it's an isolated incident or a systemic problem, it's stressful! The good news is that you can learn how to increase cash flow in your business and avoid this challenge in the first place. All you need is foresight, creativity and a dash of financial wizardry.

Remember that you'll need to refine your approach to suit your business and the economy. I work with clients to diagnose and resolve cash flow issues daily as part of my fractional CFO services, but it's not a one-size-fits-all situation.

Case Study:
What Happens When Cash is Not Proactively Managed

I had a client that was in the SaaS industry. While they were a relatively early-stage company, they had some marquis clients and provided other services to fund their product development expenses. Early on in my work with this company, it became clear that the CEO could not/ would not sit down and forecast what their cash position would be in 3–6 months. Like many entrepreneurs, he was overly optimistic in his ability to close new sales as well as collect the associated cash payments from new clients and even existing clients. Until we put in a proper weekly cash plan, he was flying by the seat of his pants and often had to delay vendor payments, defer hiring new employees, terminate contractors and more. We spent more time cleaning up the mess he had created than it would have taken to put in the proper cash planning tool.

What is Cash Flow?

"Cash flow" refers to the amount of cash your business generates in a particular period (i.e. the money in your company's bank account). Sources include customer payments or funds raised from lenders or investors. Uses include paying employees, suppliers and lenders. This cash may be in checking or savings accounts, or even short-term investments, as long as it's readily accessible.

Cash flow isn't the same as profitability. Profitability refers to financial gain from business activities, but this isn't necessarily cash in the bank. You can be profitable by selling more than you spent, but if you have to wait 30–90 days for customers to pay, you can still have a cash flow problem.

How to Increase Cash Flow: 10 Actionable Tips

Tip 1: Build a Cash Flow Forecast

One of the key aspects of monitoring cash flow is a cash flow forecast. This forecast projects your future cash inflows and outflows based on your expected sales, expenses and other financial activities. By comparing your actual cash flow to your forecast, you can identify any discrepancies and adjust your financial strategies accordingly. This proactive approach can help you avoid cash shortages and make more informed decisions about investing in your business.

The first step is building a cash flow forecast that projects your future financial position based on anticipated revenues and expenses. This provides visibility into your monthly or weekly cash position, letting you identify times of positive or negative cash flow and prepare accordingly.

Basic steps include:

- Perform an in-depth analysis of your current financial position.
- Consider your plans for the next 12 months in terms of profit and loss.
- Forecast out your balance sheet, capturing everything that will involve an inflow or outflow of cash.

- Combine your profit and loss plans with your forecasted balance sheet to get a complete picture of your expected cash flow month-to-month or week-to-week.

Once created, compare the actual performance to your monthly forecast and adjust as needed.

Tip 2: Renegotiate Terms with Vendors and Suppliers

When you're trying to figure out how to increase cash flow in your business, one of the more impactful things you can do is to renegotiate contracts with vendors and suppliers, reducing your operating expenses. Although it may not be possible with everyone, a quick review of your records may unearth some opportunities. Here are a few examples:

- <u>Rental Agreements</u>: You might offer to extend a lease in exchange for reduced rent.
- <u>Supplier Terms</u>: Ask for discounts in exchange for larger orders or longer commitments.
- <u>Utility Providers</u>: Request reductions to the best rates available.

The trick with any of these scenarios is to come to the table prepared to make an offer. Review your records and do the research so you can present comparable data. Then make your case in the spirit of "let's create a win-win." In other words, explain that you're a good customer and you want to continue working with them, but you need something in return.

Tip 3: Build a Strong Receivables Management Process

It's surprising how many companies lack a good process for collecting payments. I've seen services businesses, for instance, that do fantastic work for their clients, but bill in arrears then completely fail to follow up on late payments. Clearly, this will inhibit your cash flow. So, when solving weekly or monthly cash flow concerns, I recommend developing a rock-solid, repeatable process for accounts receivable management. This typically involves:

- Investing in Invoicing Software: Use accounting solutions that track finances and alert you to past-due invoices.
- Imposing Late Payment Penalties: Set clear payment deadlines and penalties (like 1.5% monthly) to encourage timely payment.

Although such structure may feel unnatural at first, after a few months you'll get into a groove and your clients will undoubtedly understand that this is a necessary part of doing business.

Tip 4: Take Advantage of Customer Financing Models

On the flip side of managing receivables are payment models and practices that make it easier for you to collect payment sooner. This form of financing serves to increase cash flow for you and should not be confused with extended payment terms that protect your customers' cash flow. There are a few basic ways to go about this:

- Accept Credit Cards: Process payments within 2–3 days instead of waiting a month for checks. The 3% transaction cost can often be passed to customers.
- Pre-Payment Discounts: Offer reduced rates for early or upfront payments (like "2/10 net 30" terms).
- Invoice Factoring: Sell invoices to third parties for immediate capital, eliminating collection hassles for a small fee.

Tip 5: Consider Strategic Debt

Although it's often preferable (and less stressful) to run your business debt-free, we'd encourage you to keep an open mind, especially when you're trying to decide how to increase cash flow. In short, debt financing is fine if you can afford it, meaning you should be able to service both the debt and the interest comfortably. Avoid debt, however, if you will only be able to pay the interest.

This is one of those times when your cash flow forecast (see Tip 1) will come in handy. Use it to model the impact of taking out a loan on your current and future cash flows. This will help you to see how long you'll be paying off debt and how the influx of funds will affect your ability to drive revenue. This insight will help you make such decisions with confidence.

Whether your debt comes in the form of credit cards, a line of credit from a financial institution or even long-term loans from friends and family, the important thing is to be clear on the terms. Secured loans (those based on the assets of the business or a personal guarantee) are much less expensive (6%–7% interest rates) than unsecured loans. Unsecured loans can range anywhere from 8%–10% for bank loans to 25%–35% for non-traditional lenders. And beware of lenders that build oppressive performance terms and conditions into their agreements that can put your business at risk.

Tip 6: Eliminate Non-Essential Expenses

When things are going well it's easy to overlook excess expenses. But when you begin to experience cash flow problems, you no longer have this luxury. When seeking ways to increase cash flow, you must go through your expenses with a fine-tooth comb in search of fluff. This doesn't have to be as painful as it sounds, there are often some easy opportunities that appear naturally as you build your cash flow forecast. Here are some common areas of waste to look for:

- Non-critical investments
- Deferrable professional development expenses
- Unnecessary travel and meals
- Trimmable employee perks

Explain to your team that improving cash flow helps avoid more drastic measures like downsizing.

Tip 7: Sell Ancillary Services

One of the most exciting ways to increase cash flow is to bolster your revenues by expanding your offering. For example, imagine that you manufacture and sell widgets that are used in the production of larger products. You might offer consulting services to your customers whereby you help them incorporate your widgets more effectively into their overall product line. This would be a valuable service to your customers as it would help them produce the end product in a more cost-efficient manner and would allow you to charge more.

Of course, it's important to avoid overextending yourself. Focus on products or services that complement your current offering to avoid straying too far from your core competency. Also, since cash flow is a concern, avoid anything that would add costs you can't easily absorb. Other ideas for the widget manufacturer would be to extend the product line by offering complementary products or expand into another target market using the same product line.

Tip 8: Increase Prices/Fees

One thing we look at when our clients ask us how to increase cash flow is pricing. If you've been underpricing your products or services or haven't raised your rates in several years, there may be an opportunity to impose an increase. Alternatively, you could look for ways to add value to your current offer so you can justify charging more.

This is a delicate topic, especially during an economic downturn. If you're in a competitive space, you can't afford to price yourself out of the market. And you certainly don't want to scare off loyal customers with a significant bump in cost. But if you can find a way to explain the increase it's worth exploring.

The important thing is to be transparent about the change. During the pandemic, some restaurants, for example, charged a temporary "Covid fee" to offset the cost of complying with new regulations. Most customers understood and deemed this reasonable. If you haven't raised your rates in several years, mention this in your communication to clients. Explain that you value their business, but to keep up with inflation you must occasionally raise your rates.

Tip 9: Explore New Sales and Marketing Channels

Spending more on marketing and sales probably isn't the first thing that comes to mind when you're looking for ways to increase cash flow, but bear with me. Sometimes there are hidden benefits to a change in the economy. You may have more time, underutilized resources or simply a different perspective. Whatever the case, it occasionally makes sense to explore things that are counterintuitive. Instead of conserving cash, for instance, you might consider shifting funds from one initiative to another to strengthen your position in the market. Here are a few ideas:

- **Search Engine Optimization (SEO) Investment**: Reallocate advertising funds to SEO content for long-term returns.
- **Partnership Building**: Use available time to strengthen network connections.
- **Technology Upgrades**: Ensure you can handle increased demand with better CRM systems and automated processes.

Tip 10: Establish Weekly Financial Metrics Reporting

Of course, if you're going to put forth all this effort, you must be diligent about tracking results. But how do you determine which metrics and reports are right for you? By asking yourself some important questions:

- What, exactly, do you wish to achieve in the coming months?
- Which metrics would show success?
- Which metrics can you watch to get insight into your progress?
- Do you have the right systems and processes in place to accurately measure results?
- Do you have the capability to make sense of this data and to use it to get the insights you need to make sound financial decisions?

I realize, this is my last tip, but it's important. Developing a strong, reliable system for measuring the impact of your initiatives takes some effort, but it's crucial toward ensuring success.

AI Tip

Use AI to predict customer payment behavior and identify potential cash flow issues 30-60 days before they occur. AI analyzes historical payment patterns, customer communication, and external factors to forecast when customers might pay late or need payment plan adjustments.

Key Takeaways

- **Cash flow is your business's lifeline.** Profitability means little if you can't pay suppliers or employees. For small and medium businesses, cash flow directly impacts your ability to operate and grow.

- **Proactively managing cash flow pays off.** Some cash flow improvements are simple, while others require more effort. Investing the time now can prevent crises later.

- **Take action to improve cash flow.** Create a weekly cash flow forecast, tighten your order-to-cash process, increase prices (when possible), explore new revenue streams and consider vendor or customer financing if needed.

- **Financial clarity leads to confident decisions.** With a strong handle on cash flow, you can make strategic moves from a position of strength instead of reacting to financial stress.

AI Key Takeaway Addition

Predict cash flow challenges with AI. AI-powered payment prediction helps identify potential cash flow issues weeks in advance, enabling proactive management rather than reactive problem-solving.

Once you're managing cash effectively, it's time to turn your attention to financial reporting—how to track and understand what's really happening in your business.

CHAPTER 7

Financial Reporting

A ccurate financial reporting communicates vital information about a company's economic activities to business leaders, investors and regulatory agencies. Below, I've provided an overview of financial reporting, its purpose and examples of key reports, along with tips for developing an effective reporting process.

What is Financial Reporting?

Financial reporting is the practice of capturing, organizing and delivering critical information about a company's business activities and financial performance to key stakeholders each month, quarter and year. Accountants compile details about your account balances, financial obligations and cash flows into standardized reports. Your finance team should then analyze the data and combine it with projections to develop actionable insights.

Financial reporting is necessary for businesses of every size. Small companies can operate with basic internal reporting from accounting, but organizations with complex operations or growth ambitions need more sophisticated approaches.

Reputable financial professionals follow specific rules and standards when generating reports. In the United States, most adhere to Generally Accepted Accounting Principles (GAAP), while companies outside the U.S. typically follow International Financial Reporting Standards (IFRS).

What is the Objective of Financial Reporting?

The primary purpose of financial reporting is to provide crucial insights to your executive team for effective decision-making while capturing the financial data you must share with external entities. However, that is a simple answer to a complex question. Let's look at the many ways you can use your financial information.

Track Your Company's Current Financial Health

Basic financial reporting provides visibility into where you have been and the current state of your company's finances. When your executive team reviews this data each month, they should be able to answer critical questions that will help them run the business, given the current condition of your operations, such as the following.

- Is our company profitable?
- Have we hit objectives set forth by investors or lenders?
- How are we managing growth?
- Are we promptly collecting receivables?
- Is our financial structure healthy?

Forecast Trends and Prepare for the Future

Knowing how your company is doing today is undoubtedly helpful. Yet the real power of financial reporting lies in analyzing the trends and combining the data with projections to spot problems or opportunities. In other words, you can use the data to predict where you are heading compared to your goals and address potential issues before they occur, making it easier to keep your company on track. For instance, savvy business leaders use this approach to answer questions like these.

- When will we become profitable?
- Are we on track to hit revenue targets?
- Will we stay within budget?
- Do we have enough cash for upcoming obligations?
- Can we fulfill potential new business?

Analyze the Potential of Proposed Initiatives

Once you have built in projections, you can run what-if scenarios to model potential effects of proposed initiatives, such as:

- Should we borrow more for investments?
- Do we need to raise outside capital?
- Can we afford an acquisition or market expansion?
- What's the best growth strategy?
- How long until we see returns on investments?

Communicate Important Data to Company Stakeholders

It is not only leadership that needs financial information. Other internal and external stakeholders also rely on this data. For example, department heads and certain managers will use financial data to inform decisions about discrete areas of your business, and employees look to company performance for motivation. A healthy business suggests career and earnings potential, especially if your compensation plans include profit sharing or equity.

External stakeholders, such as current and potential investors and creditors, also evaluate a company's financial position. Indeed, some expect upfront and regular reporting throughout the relationship. You may need to share financial data with vendors, suppliers or customers to assure them that you can meet your obligations. And finally, let's not forget about your Board of Directors, which will expect high-level reporting and insights at quarterly board meetings.

Manage Compliance with Regulatory Agencies

The data generated by financial reporting will also help you meet the legal obligations of doing business. For example, the Internal Revenue Service (IRS) requires that you submit these details when filing taxes. You may also be subject to financial reporting requirements from industry-specific regulatory organizations.

Public companies must file reports with the Securities and Exchange Commission (SEC), including financial disclosures. Many produce formal annual reports detailing their performance and activities, regardless of regulations.

Given the usefulness of these reports, developing a watertight financial reporting process is in every company's best interest. So, what types of financial statements should you expect from your finance and accounting team?

What Types of Financial Reports Do You Need?

Financial reporting occurs in a monthly, quarterly and yearly cycle, and the contents of each statement can vary depending on the audience. For example, potential lenders typically do not consider financial projections during underwriting. Instead, they rely on a high-level snapshot of your current financial situation and historical track record to determine your ability to repay the debt. Therefore, an appropriate financial reporting package for a lender would only include your income statement, balance sheet and statement of cash flows for the past 2–3 years.

Let's look at examples of these three critical statements.

Income Statement

The income statement (a.k.a. profit and loss or P&L statement) shows the breakdown of your organization's revenues and expenses for a certain period of time and how that translates into net profits (or losses). It is a simple report with subtotals for gross profit (revenue minus cost of revenues) and operating income (gross profit minus operating expenses), with a final tally for net income (operating income minus other income and expenses). This report provides insight into the company's productivity and profitability. Many also use the income statement to benchmark the company's performance against other organizations.

Acme Tech, Inc.

Profit & Loss Statement

	Current Year	Prior Year	Variance $	Variance %
Revenue				
Services	$ 2,220,863	$ 2,885,774	$ (664,912)	-23%
Sales	$ 3,091,499	$ 2,651,226	$ 440,273	17%
Total Revenue	**$ 5,312,362**	**$ 5,537,001**	**$ (224,639)**	**-4%**
Cost of Goods Sold				
Direct Labor	$ 1,175,002	$ 1,549,013	$ (374,011)	-24%
Software - COGS	$ 2,017,491	$ 381,086	$ 1,636,405	429%
Subcontractors	$ 286,140	$ 561,253	$ (275,113)	-49%
Total Cost of Goods Sold	**$ 3,478,633**	**$ 2,491,353**	**$ 987,281**	**40%**
Operating Margin $	$ 1,833,729	$ 3,045,648	$ (1,211,919)	-40%
Operating Margin %	35%	55%		
SG&A Costs				
General & Administrative	$ 429,667	$ 706,875	$ (277,208)	-39%
Professional Fees	$ 238,486	$ 324,775	$ (86,289)	-27%
Research & Development	$ 1,328,331	$ 1,502,154	$ (173,823)	-12%
Sales & Marketing	$ 611,253	$ 251,342	$ 359,910	143%
Total SG&A Costs	**$ 2,607,736**	**$ 2,785,146**	**$ (177,410)**	**-6%**
Net Operating Income	**$ (774,008)**	**$ 260,502**	**$ (1,034,510)**	**-397%**
Other Income				
ESI Rimbursed Expenses	$ 447,450	$ -	$ 447,450	n/m
Total Other Income	**$ 447,450**	**$ -**	**$ 447,450**	**n/m**
Other Expenses				
Depreciation Expense	$ 21,627	$ 21,308	$ 319	1%
Income Taxes	$ 3,492	$ 6,659	$ (3,167)	-48%
Interest Expense	$ 23,552	$ 3,643	$ 19,909	546%
Other Expense	$ -	$ 100,000	$ (100,000)	-100%
Sales Tax	$ -	$ 8,156	$ (8,156)	-100%
Total Other Expenses	**$ 48,671**	**$ 139,766**	**$ (91,095)**	**-65%**
Pre-tax Income	**$ (375,229)**	**$ 120,736**	**$ (495,965)**	**-411%**

Balance Sheet

In contrast, a company's balance sheet documents an organization's total assets, liabilities and shareholder's equity. It is a combination of investment made into the business and profits earned to date, i.e., retained earnings, as reported on the income statement. It provides a snapshot of where things stand at a particular point in time. Put another way, it shows how much you have and owe and the company's net worth on a specific date.

As a stand-alone document, this report speaks volumes. For instance, potential investors and creditors can use it to see whether you have a healthy balance of debt vs. equity or if you are an investment risk. They can also combine it with other financial statements to evaluate your company's financial stability.

Acme Tech, Inc.

Balance Sheet

	Month End
Assets	
Cash	$ 609,005
Accounts Receivable	$ 1,529,348
Prepaid expenses	$ 367,712
Fixed Assets	$ 131,781
Other Assets	$ 66,022
Total Assets	**$ 2,703,868**
Liabilities	
Accounts Payable	$ 475,571
Credit card payables	$ 35,564
Other Current Liabilities	$ 1,330,123
Notes payable	$ 627,762
Liabilities Subtotal	**$ 2,469,020**

Equity

Common Stock	$	1,000
Paid in Capital	$	770,720
Retained Earnings	$	(704,358)
Shareholder Distributions	$	-
Net Income	$	167,486
Equity Subtotal	**$**	**234,849**

Total Liabilities & Equity	**$ 2,703,868**

Statement of Cash Flows

The cash flow statement (a.k.a. the statement of cash flows) shows how and when money flows into and out of the business. It connects the income statement and balance sheet to show all sources and uses of cash, broken down into three main areas.

- Operating Activities – changes in cash due to essential operations.
- Investment Activities – cash movement from paying for or selling the equipment or other assets you need to run your business (if any).
- Financing Activities – cash flow from obtaining credit, an equity investment, making dividend payments or paying off loans.

The statement of cash flows is less helpful than the prior two reports without more context, but those with financial acumen can still glean insights.

Acme Tech, Inc.

Statement of Cash Flows

	Month	YTD
Cash flows from Operating Activities		
Net income (loss)	$ 124,908	$ (184,496)
Depreciation	$ 3,090	$ 21,627
Changes in operating assets & liabilities		
Increase in accounts receivable	$ (6,338,075)	$ (6,075,499)
Increase in prepaid expenses	$ (1,089,848)	$ (1,062,408)
Increase in accounts payable	$ 61,851	$ 1,902,513
Increase in credit card payables	$ 2,950	$ (18,344)
Increase in other payables	$ 6,705,124	$ 6,620,580
Short-term loan payments	$ (5,667)	$ (25,009)
Total cash from Operating Activities	$ (663,665)	$ 1,341,833
Cash flows from Investing activities	$ -	$ (502,731)
Cash flows from Financing activities	$ -	$ 674,300
Net increase (decrease) in cash	$ (535,667)	$ 1,350,533
Beginning Cash	$ 2,211,328	$ 325,127
Ending Cash	$ 1,675,661	$ 1,675,660

The
CEO's
RIGHT HAND

Remember, the reports above are just a start. Other financial statements can also be helpful, depending on the business. For instance, accounts receivable and accounts payable aging reports can be quite telling for companies that sell business-to-business. These organizations must be mindful of bills and invoices that sit on the books for too long, putting the company at risk of cash flow problems.

How Does Financial Reporting Evolve with Your Business?

As your company matures, your executive team or board will need more information. They will need comprehensive financial reporting, including current and historical financial data analysis, projections and insights to guide decision-making. That will empower the team with the information necessary to grow and scale the business. Reporting packages for executives or boards will likely include the three statements above (modified to include a comparison to historical data), reports specific to the business and the following information.

Executive Summary

An executive summary typically precedes any financial reporting documents presented to executive teams, boards or shareholders. It is a written financial analysis that describes what has happened since the last report (as revealed in the numbers) and the finance team's recommendations.

Prepared for **Acme Tech, Inc.**

Financial Reporting Package

The CEO's RIGHT HAND

CONTENTS

Financial Summary

2	Balance Sheet
3	P&L Trend
4	Statement of Cash Flows

Key Performance Indicators

5	A R Aging Summary
6	High Level Budget - Progress to Forecast
7	Sales by Client

KEY TAKEAWAYS & ACTION ITEMS

Overall, Acme's position is strong heading into the current year.

Recent Wins:
- First, we have been able to deliver on the massive project backlog for which we received payment up-front. This has greatly reduced our accounts payable liability.
- We have nearly achieved our gross profit goal of 70%. We are confident we will achieve this goal in the next two quarters.
- Our debt reduction efforts have been paying off resulting in a reduction of the bank facility by $232K.
- Both items above have contributed to an increase of $322K in working capital; as a reminder, we used to be in a negative working capital position! This is great news.
- 89.6% of receivables are current and/or under 60 days overdue.
- While we had a slow start to the year, we are still 30% over last year's revenues year-to-date.

Items that require attention / discussion:
- The product side of the business continues to generate margins below 10%. We recommend discussing if shutting this division makes sense.
- There are virtually no repeat customers in 2022 vs. 2021. This presents a challenge for the business, as we must rely on new lead generation. Let's discuss opportunities to increase repeat purchases.
- Our close rate is slightly below projections, and may impact our ability to hit our growth targets. We recommend that the CEO get more involved in closing business opportunities until we determine a strategy for moving business through the funnel more efficiently.

As always, thank you for partnering with us at The CEO's Right Hand. We greatly enjoy being part of the Acme family.

KPI Dashboard

A Key Performance Indicator (KPI) dashboard is a one-page document that displays high-level metrics about a company's performance. It provides quick insight into whether the business is on track to achieve its goals, enabling you to spot and address issues before they spiral out of control. I recommend limiting the KPI dashboard to a few areas, like the example in the next chapter. But don't let its simplicity fool you. This critical report summarizes your most important financial data. Update the numbers every month or quarter to keep them accurate and useful.

Cash Flow Forecast

A cash flow forecast is a detailed report that shows your company's current cash position and a projection of its future cash position based on anticipated revenues and expenses. This document complements and extends your statement of cash flows report by forecasting the future, making the data more valuable and actionable. It can help you avoid any cash flow problems that might inhibit your ability to run the business.

Acme Services, LLC
Weekly Cash Forecast

Week Ending	14-Mar	21-Mar	28-Mar	04-Apr	11-Apr	18-Apr	25-Apr	02-May
OPERATING CASH IN								
Account Receivables Collected	37,294	54,003	-	20,334	-	27,968	76,179	50,347
Other Cash Received	966							
Total Operating Cash In	$ 38,259	$ 54,003	$ -	$ 20,334	$ -	$ 27,968	$ 76,179	$ 50,347
OPERATING CASH OUT								
Consulting	67,638	15,000	-	10,000	-	10,000	-	10,000
Product	16,500							
Marketing	-	-	-	2,500	-	2,500	-	2,500
Accounting/IT/Legal	10,000	3,179	-	7,523	-	-	-	10,000
Internal								
Salaries & Bonuses	25,407	-	25,407	-	16,674	-	16,674	-
Credit Card Payments	-	-	5,000	-	-	5,000	-	-
Insurance & Bank Fees	-	-	2,152	-	-	2,152	-	-
Other	327	-	10,000	-	-	10,000	-	-
Travel & Other reimbursements	-	-	2,000	-	-	2,000	-	-
Owner's Draw	-	-	9,000	-	-	18,000	-	-
Contractors	-	5,000	-	-	-	5,000	-	-
Total Operating Cash Out	$ 119,872	$ 23,179	$ 53,560	$ 20,023	$ 16,674	$ 54,652	$ 16,674	$ 22,500
Net Operating Cashflow	$ (81,613)	$ 30,825	$ (53,560)	$ 310	$ (16,674)	$(26,684)	$ 59,505	$ 27,847
Total Non-Operating Cashflow	$ -	$ (10,463)	$ -	$ -	$ (8,879)	$ (1,583)	$ -	$ -
TOTAL CASHFLOW	$ (81,613)	$ 20,362	$ (53,560)	$ 310	$ (25,552)	$(28,267)	$ 59,505	$ 27,847
BEGINNING CASH BALANCE	$222,207	$140,595	$160,957	$107,397	$107,707	$ 82,155	$ 53,888	$113,393
END OF PERIOD CASH BALANCE	$140,595	$160,957	$107,397	$107,707	$ 82,155	$ 53,888	$113,393	$141,240

AI Tip

Implement AI-powered variance analysis that automatically explains significant changes in your financial reports. Instead of manually investigating why expenses increased or revenue declined, AI can identify the root causes and present explanations in plain English, saving hours of analysis time.

Key Takeaways

- **Clear reporting drives better decisions.** Financial reporting gives CEOs the visibility they need to understand the company's health and take timely, informed action.

- **Each report serves a distinct purpose.** The income statement tracks profitability, the balance sheet reveals financial position and the cash flow statement shows liquidity.

- **Reporting evolves with growth.** As your business matures, your reporting must mature too—adding insights, historical comparisons, KPIs and executive summaries.

- **Forecasting makes reporting actionable.** Use financial reports in tandem with forecasts and what-if scenarios to guide strategic planning and avoid cash shortfalls.

- **Stakeholders rely on your numbers.** Reliable reports build confidence with lenders, investors, board members and your internal leadership team.

- **Consistent reporting creates accountability.** Monthly financial packages with dashboards and variance analysis help teams stay aligned and focused on results.

AI Key Takeaway Addition

Accelerate reporting with AI automation. AI can automatically generate financial reports, perform variance analysis, and provide explanations for significant changes, reducing reporting time from weeks to days.

Financial reports give you the data. KPIs help you focus on what matters. Now, let's break down how to use performance indicators to guide your decisions.

CHAPTER 8

Key Performance Indicators

To run a business effectively, you must rise above day-to-day operations and take a big picture view. You need to know what's going well, what needs attention and how to prioritize. Tools like a KPI dashboard make this easier.

What is a KPI?

A Key Performance Indicator (KPI) is a high-level measure of a particular aspect of your business that quickly shows whether your company is on track to meet its goals. While a KPI is a metric, not all metrics are KPIs. Your organization uses various metrics to gauge success, but KPIs are the most critical ones that measure overall business performance, provide actionable insights, and inform decisions.

Revenue is an obvious KPI—if you're at risk of missing revenue goals, you must investigate and find solutions. Other high-level KPIs include operational metrics (like customer acquisition rates) and financial metrics from your accounting system (like profit). The challenge is narrowing your focus to the most meaningful metrics for your KPI dashboard.

What is a KPI Dashboard?

A key performance indicator dashboard is a visualization of your KPIs designed for easy consumption. When data is digestible, you feel less overwhelmed and can quickly assess your company's health, spot problems and address them before they escalate. Many business leaders display KPIs using color-coding, with red indicating problem areas and green showing success. This draws the eye to numbers that matter, giving you an at-a-glance view of business performance.

What is the Purpose of a KPI Dashboard?

A KPI dashboard is an easy-to-use tool for monitoring your company's performance, clearly showing when your business is thriving and when it needs work. In our example dashboard, we've limited the focus to six areas, each with one or more KPIs. We recommend keeping this report to just a handful of functional areas to maintain usefulness.

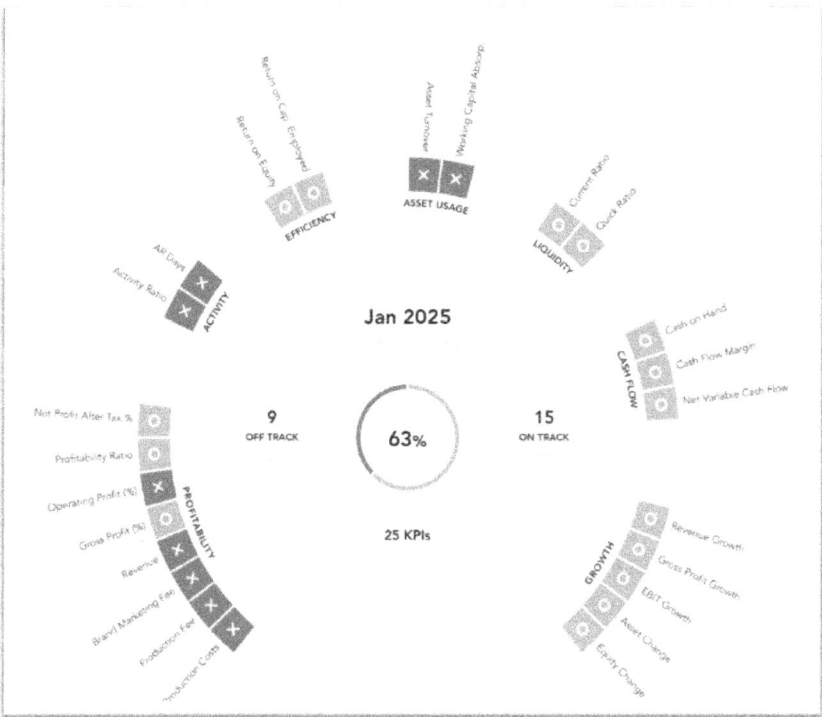

For instance, the Growth KPIs section includes Revenue Growth, EBIT Growth, Gross Profit Growth, etc.—all green in this example, indicating strong performance. However, the Profitability KPIs show underperformance, with five of eight KPIs in red.

Ideally, you'll also use your dashboard as a benchmark, comparing your company with industry competitors. Notable differences are red flags that warrant investigation.

Should You Have a KPI Dashboard for Every Department Leader?

Our example of the executive dashboard was developed with the CEO in mind, which is typically sufficient for small to medium-sized businesses. As your company grows and becomes more complex, you might create dashboards for each department leader.

You could implement operational, marketing, customer satisfaction and human resources dashboards. Each department leader can identify their KPIs to show how their group's performance contributes to company goals.

When your organization needs deeper insight, it may be time to invest in a business intelligence solution like Tableau or Microsoft Power BI. These data visualization tools consolidate information and provide access to underlying numbers, potentially in real time. However, these tools are expensive, so most growing companies start with a simple Excel spreadsheet.

How to Build a KPI Dashboard

The process will vary between companies and become more involved as your business grows. Generally, these are the basic steps:

1. **Build a Strong Financial and Operational Model** – Create a detailed month-by-month model with underlying data that will feed your KPI dashboard. Capture everything about current and anticipated revenue and expenses, including influencing factors like marketing and sales activities. With smaller companies, this is typically done in a spreadsheet or using a reporting tool. Project financial results for the next twelve months based on historical data and trends.

2. **Set Goals** – Determine short and long-term targets needed to keep your business on track. These numbers will gauge your

performance each month. Be optimistic but realistic about your capabilities.

3. **Identify Potential KPIs** – Determine which metrics are candidates for your dashboard. These should be high-level, important metrics that demonstrate business health and help your management team pursue strategic goals. They must be actionable—you should have solutions ready if you're at risk of missing targets.

Many clients use the "SMART" framework to narrow possibilities, ensuring each potential KPI is Specific, Measurable, Achievable, Realistic and Timely. Once you have a list of candidates, discuss until you agree on the 3–6 most important ones.

1. **Review Your Historical Data for Those KPIs** – Examine your data sources for tracking KPIs. Can you see trends, or do you need to implement systems to access this information?
2. **Build the KPI Dashboard** – Create a new sheet in your financial model spreadsheet. Design it to automatically pull necessary information from underlying numbers and update monthly when new data is added. This should be a one-page, easy-to-understand sheet allowing you to quickly spot issues.

After completing this process, update your numbers monthly. Your executive team will develop a rhythm of reviewing data, discussing its meaning and making data-driven decisions.

Which KPIs Should You Track for Your Business?

Selecting the right KPIs depends on your industry, company maturity and business model. While knowing what others use can help, you'll need a customized dashboard. Most businesses track some variation of:

- Revenue Growth
- Gross Margins
- Net Income

However, specific calculations differ by industry and business model. Here are examples:

KPIs for SaaS or Subscription-Based Industries

When building on customer relationships with compounding earnings, you track different metrics:

- **Monthly/Annual Recurring Revenue (MRR/ARR)** – SaaS companies focus heavily on growing recurring revenues, which are more valuable than one-time revenues.
- **Lifetime Value of a Customer (LTV)** – The total revenue a customer is expected to generate throughout their relationship with your company.
- **Customer Acquisition Costs (CAC)** – Total marketing expense required to source new customers.
- **Churn Rate** – Percentage of customers lost over a period.

You might combine KPIs into ratios for deeper insights. For instance, LTV:CAC provides insight into profitability and efficiency, with an ideal ratio of at least 4:1.

Ecommerce Business KPIs

Businesses selling relatively low-cost items online rely on volume and marketing to drive new and repeat business:

- **Average Order Value (AOV)** – Average dollar size of orders over time.
- **Churn Rate** – Rate at which you lose customers.
- **Lifetime Value** – How long customers remain and how much they spend during their journey.
- **Gross Margin** – Profit generated from selling goods or services.
- **Return On Ad Spend (ROAS)** – Effectiveness of advertising investments.

KPIs for Companies that Provide Business Services

For service-based businesses relying on human capital:

- **Billable Hours** – Time spent on client work versus administration.
- **Gross Profit Per Client** – Remaining profit after subtracting human capital and overhead costs.
- **Churn Rate** – Client retention duration.
- **Capacity and Capacity Utilization** – Efficiency of time usage.

AI Tip

Set up AI-powered KPI monitoring that tracks your key metrics continuously and sends alerts when performance deviates from targets. This proactive approach ensures you address problems immediately rather than discovering them during monthly reviews when correction opportunities may be limited.

Key Takeaways

- **Track only the most impactful KPIs.** Not all metrics matter. Focus on 3–6 key indicators that directly influence decisions and align with business goals.

- **Keep dashboards simple and actionable.** A well-designed KPI dashboard should provide clear, at-a-glance insights that help guide strategy without unnecessary complexity.

- **Continuously refine your KPIs.** As your business evolves, regularly assess and adjust KPIs to ensure they stay relevant and support growth.

- **Use data to make smarter decisions.** Up-to-date, visualized KPIs allow you to spot trends, address issues proactively and align your team around key objectives.

AI Key Takeaway Addition

Monitor KPIs continuously with AI alerts. Automated monitoring systems provide real-time alerts when key metrics deviate from targets, enabling immediate corrective action.

KPIs give you snapshots. Now it's time to bring it all together—reports, trends and insights—to make smart, forward-looking decisions.

CHAPTER 9

Strategic Financial Performance Monitoring and Decision Making

For small-business CEOs, the ability to monitor financial performance and make strategic financial decisions is a critical skill that directly impacts growth, profitability and long-term sustainability. Many CEOs excel at creating products or delivering services but struggle to translate financial data into actionable insights that drive their business forward. This chapter explores how effective financial monitoring and decision-making processes can transform raw financial data into a powerful strategic advantage.

Tracking and Evaluating Financial Performance

Effective financial monitoring begins with establishing clear metrics tied to your strategic objectives. While profitability and cash flow are fundamental concerns for any business, the specific indicators that provide the most valuable insights will vary based on your industry, business model and growth stage.

Setting Meaningful Financial Goals and Metrics

Financial goals should be both aspirational and realistic, providing clear targets that energize your team while remaining achievable. The most effective financial goals follow the SMART framework—specific, measurable, achievable, relevant and time-bound.

When establishing financial metrics, focus on a balanced mix of:

- **Leading indicators** that predict future performance (sales pipeline, customer acquisition rates, marketing qualified leads)
- **Lagging indicators** that measure historical results (revenue, profit margins, cash flow)
- **Efficiency metrics** that evaluate operational effectiveness (customer acquisition cost, inventory turnover, employee productivity)

For instance, a professional services firm might track metrics like billable utilization rate, average hourly rate, project profitability and client retention rate, while a SaaS company would prioritize monthly recurring revenue (MRR), customer lifetime value (LTV), customer acquisition cost (CAC) and churn rate.

Case Study:
Setting the Right Metrics for Growth

One of our manufacturing clients was frustrated by their stagnant growth despite consistent profitability. Their management team religiously monitored revenue, gross margin and net profit but struggled to understand why sales weren't accelerating. When we began working together, we discovered they had no metrics tracking their sales pipeline, market penetration or customer satisfaction.

We implemented a new dashboard that maintained their profitability metrics while adding key leading indicators like qualified opportunities, quote-to-close ratio and net promoter score. Within three months, they identified that their sales team was generating sufficient leads, but the quote-to-close ratio was significantly below industry standards. This insight led to targeted sales training and process improvements that increased their conversion rate by 35% within six months, directly accelerating revenue growth.

Building a Comprehensive Financial Monitoring System

To track financial performance effectively, you need more than occasional reviews of standalone reports. A strong monitoring system integrates data collection, analysis and presentation to deliver timely insights for informed decision-making.

Key components of an effective financial monitoring system include:

1. **Consistent Reporting Cadence** – Close monthly financials within 10–15 days and distribute reports promptly to key stakeholders.
2. **Financial Dashboard** – A single-page visual summary of critical KPIs for quick performance assessment.
3. **Variance Analysis** – Regularly compare actual results to budgets and forecasts to pinpoint discrepancies and their causes.
4. **Trend Analysis** – Track key financial metrics over time to identify patterns and anticipate future shifts.
5. **Industry Benchmarking** – Compare your performance against industry standards and competitors for valuable context.

This comprehensive approach transforms financial monitoring from a backward-looking accounting exercise into a forward-looking strategic tool that supports proactive decision-making.

The Critical Role of Regular Financial Reviews

Financial data only creates value when it informs action. Establishing a structured review process ensures that financial insights translate into operational improvements and strategic adjustments.

An effective financial review process typically includes:

- **Weekly cash flow reviews** focusing on immediate liquidity and operational needs
- **Monthly management reviews** examining broader performance metrics and short-term trends
- **Quarterly strategic reviews** addressing longer-term patterns and progress toward annual goals

- **Annual planning sessions** setting targets and strategies for the coming year

During these reviews, the focus should extend beyond simply reporting numbers to understanding their implications and determining appropriate responses. Each review should conclude with clear action items assigned to specific team members with defined timelines for implementation.

Case Study:
The Power of Structured Financial Reviews

One of our retail clients, with multiple locations, struggled with inconsistent performance across their stores. Their financial reporting system generated detailed statements for each location, but managers rarely reviewed them thoroughly, focusing instead only on top-line sales.

We implemented a structured monthly review process where each store manager met with the operations director and a financial analyst to examine not just revenue but also gross margin by product category, labor efficiency, inventory shrinkage and overhead costs. Each review concluded with specific action commitments that were documented and followed up in subsequent meetings.

Within two quarters, their worst-performing store improved its operating margin by 7%, and the company identified several best practices that were subsequently implemented across all locations. The CEO later commented that these regular reviews created a "financial fluency" throughout the organization that fundamentally changed how managers approached their roles.

Making Sound Financial Decisions

Monitoring performance is important, but the real goal is using those insights to make smart decisions for your business. Strategic financial management balances data analysis with business judgment to drive growth while managing risk.

The Financial Decision-Making Framework

Effective financial decisions follow a structured approach that balances quantitative analysis with qualitative factors:

1. **Define the Objective** – Clarify what you're trying to accomplish and how it aligns with your overall strategy.
2. **Identify Alternatives** – Generate multiple potential solutions rather than considering only the obvious options.
3. **Gather Relevant Data** – Collect the financial and operational information needed to evaluate each alternative.
4. **Analyze Impacts** – Assess how each option affects your financial position, operations and strategic goals.
5. **Consider Qualitative Factors** – Evaluate non-financial implications like market positioning, employee morale and customer perception.
6. **Assess Risks** – Identify potential downsides and develop contingency plans.
7. **Make the Decision** – Select the option that best balances potential returns with acceptable risk.
8. **Implement and Monitor** – Execute your decision and track results to enable course correction if necessary.

This framework provides a consistent approach to decision-making while remaining flexible enough to accommodate the unique circumstances of each situation.

Critical Financial Decisions for Growing Businesses

Small business CEOs face a range of financial decisions as their companies evolve. The most common include:

Capital Investment Decisions

Whether you're considering new equipment, technology systems or facility expansions, capital investments require careful evaluation of both immediate costs and long-term returns.

Effective capital investment decisions should incorporate:

- **Multiple valuation methods** – Net Present Value (NPV), Internal Rate of Return (IRR) and payback period provide complementary perspectives on potential returns.
- **Sensitivity analysis** – Testing how results change under different assumptions helps identify which variables most significantly impact outcomes.
- **Opportunity cost considerations** – Evaluating what else you could do with the same capital ensures you're making the best possible use of limited resources.

Pricing Decisions

Your pricing strategy directly impacts both top-line revenue and bottom-line profitability. Strategic pricing decisions balance market positioning, customer value perception and internal cost structures.

Effective pricing decisions should consider:

- **Cost structures** – Understanding your fixed and variable costs provides a foundation for setting minimum acceptable prices.
- **Customer value perception** – Pricing should reflect the value customers receive, not just your internal costs.
- **Competitive positioning** – Your pricing strategy signals your market position relative to competitors.
- **Segmentation opportunities** – Different customer groups may have varying price sensitivities and value perceptions.

Resource Allocation Decisions

Growing businesses constantly face choices about how to allocate limited financial resources across competing priorities like marketing, product development, talent acquisition, and infrastructure improvements. Effective resource allocation decisions require:

- **Clear strategic priorities** – Resources should flow primarily to initiatives that advance your most important strategic objectives.
- **Return on investment analysis** – Comparing the expected returns from different investments helps optimize resource deployment.
- **Risk balancing** – Distributing resources across initiatives with different risk profiles creates a more resilient overall portfolio.

Case Study:
Strategic Resource Allocation in Action

Our client, a fast-growing technology services company, faced the classic dilemma of choosing between investing in sales expansion or product development. With limited capital, they couldn't adequately fund both priorities, and their leadership team was divided on which direction would create the most value.

Working with their executive team, we developed a detailed analysis comparing the projected returns from each investment path. The analysis went beyond simple revenue projections to examine contribution margins, cash flow timing and long-term strategic positioning.

The data revealed that while sales expansion would generate faster short-term revenue growth, product development investments would create significantly higher margins and more defensible market positions over a three-year horizon. Based on this analysis, the company allocated 70% of its available investment capital to product development while focusing sales efforts on higher-margin opportunities with existing capabilities.

Two years later, their revenues had grown more modestly than some competitors, but their EBITDA margin exceeded the industry average by 12%, and their valuation multiple in a subsequent funding round reflected this premium positioning.

Long-Term Financial Planning for Sustainability

While day-to-day financial decisions address immediate needs, long-term financial planning ensures your business remains sustainable and continues creating value over extended periods. Effective long-term financial planning integrates strategic vision with practical financial constraints to chart a viable path to your desired future state.

The key components of sustainable financial planning include:

Capital Structure Optimization

Your capital structure—the balance between debt and equity financing—significantly impacts both risk profile and potential returns. Too much debt increases financial vulnerability during downturns, while excessive equity dilutes ownership and potentially returns.

Optimal capital structures typically:

- **Match financing sources to asset types** – Long-term assets should be financed with long-term capital, while short-term needs can be met with more flexible funding.
- **Maintain financial flexibility** – Preserving unused borrowing capacity provides options during both challenges and opportunities.
- **Balance cost of capital with risk management** – While debt typically costs less than equity, it also increases financial risk that must be carefully managed.

Sustainable Growth Planning

Rapid growth can strain financial resources and operational capabilities, potentially creating more risk than value. Sustainable growth planning ensures your expansion ambitions align with your financial capacity.

Effective growth planning addresses:

- **Organic vs. inorganic growth** – Balancing internal development with strategic acquisitions based on capabilities and market opportunities.

- **Working capital requirements** – Anticipating how growth will impact inventory, receivables and payables to ensure adequate liquidity.
- **Infrastructure scaling** – Timing investments in physical and technological infrastructure to support growth without creating excess capacity.

Succession and Exit Planning

Even if it is not immediately relevant, having a clear vision for the eventual transition of ownership and leadership provides a North Star for long-term financial decisions.

Comprehensive succession and exit planning include:

- **Business valuation strategies** – Understanding which financial metrics most significantly impact your company's value in potential transactions.
- **Value enhancement initiatives** – Identifying and addressing factors that could limit valuation multiples in a future sale.
- **Tax-efficient transfer structures** – Exploring ownership transition approaches that maximize after-tax proceeds for all parties.

Case Study:
Exit Planning Creates Immediate Value

A successful service business owner had no immediate plans to sell but wanted to understand his options for eventual retirement. During an analysis, we identified several aspects of the business that would significantly impact valuation in a potential sale.

The business relied heavily on the owner's personal relationships with key clients, had inconsistent financial documentation and lacked standardized delivery processes that could scale without the owner's direct involvement. While extremely profitable, these characteristics would substantially reduce its value to potential acquirers.

Even though the owner planned to remain active for at least five more years, he implemented changes immediately based on the recommendations: developing a client transition plan, standardizing financial reporting practices and documenting core service delivery methodologies that others could execute.

Three years later, an unexpected acquisition offer arrived from a strategic buyer. Because of the changes already implemented, the business commanded a valuation multiple nearly 40% higher than comparable companies in the same industry. The owner had created several million dollars in additional exit value simply by making decisions with eventual transferability in mind—years before he actually planned to sell.

Integrating Financial Monitoring and Decision Making

The most successful businesses create a virtuous cycle where financial monitoring informs better decisions, which in turn produce improved financial results that appear in subsequent monitoring cycles.

This integration depends on three critical elements:

1. Financial Literacy Throughout the Organization

Financial insights create the most value when they're understood and applied by operational leaders throughout your company, not just the finance team. Developing financial literacy across your organization enables better day-to-day decisions aligned with your overall financial goals.

Strategies for building organizational financial literacy include:

- Simplified financial dashboards tailored to different functional areas
- Regular financial education sessions for managers and team leaders
- Clear connection between financial metrics and operational activities
- Celebration of financial wins to reinforce the importance of financial performance

2. Cross-Functional Collaboration

Financial decisions rarely exist in isolation; they affect and are affected by virtually every aspect of your business. Creating structured collaboration between finance and other departments ensures that financial considerations are integrated into operational planning while financial strategies reflect operational realities.

Effective cross-functional collaboration practices include:

- Joint planning sessions that bring together finance and operational leaders
- Shared accountability for financial outcomes across departments
- Regular cross-functional reviews of both financial and operational metrics
- Integrated forecasting processes that incorporate insights from all business areas

3. Continuous Improvement Mindset

Financial monitoring and decision-making processes should themselves be subject to regular evaluation and refinement. What worked for your business at $1 million in revenue may be insufficient at $10 million, requiring evolution in both the metrics you track and how you make decisions.

A continuous improvement approach to financial management includes:

- Regular assessment of which metrics provide the most valuable insights
- Refinement of reporting formats to enhance clarity and usability
- Evaluation of decision-making processes to identify improvement opportunities
- Incorporation of new analytical tools and methodologies as your business evolves

By integrating monitoring and decision-making into a cohesive financial management approach and continuously improving that approach as your business grows, you create a powerful competitive advantage that supports sustainable success.

AI Tip

Use AI to perform scenario analysis and "what-if" modeling for major business decisions. AI can quickly model dozens of potential outcomes and their financial implications, helping you evaluate strategic options more thoroughly than traditional manual analysis allows.

Key Takeaways

- **Establish clear, meaningful financial metrics** tied directly to your strategic objectives, including a balanced mix of leading indicators, lagging indicators and efficiency measures tailored to your specific business model.

- **Build a comprehensive financial monitoring system** that integrates regular reporting, dashboards, variance analysis and structured review processes to transform data into actionable insights.

- **Apply a consistent decision-making framework** that balances quantitative analysis with qualitative factors, ensuring that financial decisions align with your overall strategy while appropriately managing risk.

- **Develop long-term financial planning processes** that address capital structure optimization, sustainable growth and eventual succession or exit to ensure your business remains viable and valuable over time.

- **Create a virtuous cycle** by integrating monitoring and decision-making, building financial literacy throughout your organization, fostering cross-functional collaboration and continuously improving your financial management approach as your business evolves.

AI Key Takeaway Addition

Enhance strategic decisions with AI modeling. AI-powered scenario analysis enables rapid evaluation of multiple strategic options, improving decision quality while reducing analysis time.

With performance monitoring in place, it's time to look at how to protect your profits—and stay compliant—through smart tax planning.

PART 3

Taxes, Capital, and Investors

CHAPTER 10

Tax Planning & Compliance

As a CEO, you've likely heard the saying, "It's not what you make, but what you keep that matters." While growing revenue is essential, maximizing after-tax profits directly impacts your ability to reinvest in growth, attract investors and ultimately build business value. Yet tax planning remains one of the most overlooked aspects of financial management for small business leaders.

Many CEOs view taxes as an unavoidable burden to be handled by accountants once a year. This reactive approach not only increases your tax liability but also creates unnecessary financial stress and potential compliance risks. The most successful businesses integrate tax planning into their year-round financial strategy, turning what many see as a burden into a strategic advantage.

Understanding Your Tax Obligations

Before diving into strategies, let's clarify the primary tax obligations facing small businesses. Depending on your entity structure, industry and location, you'll likely encounter some combination of the following:

Income Taxes

As a business owner, you'll face income taxes at both the business and personal levels. How this works depends on your business structure:

- **Sole Proprietorships, Partnerships and S Corporations**: These "pass-through" entities don't pay taxes at the business level. Instead, profits flow to your personal tax return, where they're taxed at your individual rate. While this avoids double taxation, it can create a significant personal tax burden during profitable years.

- **C Corporations**: These entities pay corporate income tax on profits (currently 21% at the federal level). If you then distribute dividends to yourself as a shareholder, those distributions are taxed again on your personal return, creating potential double taxation.

Employment Taxes

If you have employees (including yourself), you're responsible for:

- **Social Security and Medicare (FICA)**: Employers must withhold 7.65% of employee wages and match this amount for a total of 15.3%.
- **Federal and State Unemployment (FUTA/SUTA)**: These taxes fund unemployment benefits and typically apply to the first $7,000–$10,000 of each employee's wages.
- **Income Tax Withholding**: You must withhold federal and applicable state and local income taxes from employee paychecks.

Case Study:
The Costly Mistake of Misclassifying Workers

I once worked with a service-based client who decided to classify all their workers as independent contractors rather than employees to "save on taxes." When the IRS audited them, they faced over $200,000 in back taxes, penalties and interest. We helped implement a proper classification system and negotiated with the IRS, but this costly mistake could have been avoided with proper planning.

Sales and Use Tax

If you sell taxable products or services, you'll need to collect and remit sales tax based on the jurisdictions where you have "nexus" (a significant business presence). With the 2018 Supreme Court decision in *South Dakota v. Wayfair*, even companies without a physical presence may be required to collect sales tax in states where they have economic nexus.

Property Tax

If your business owns real estate or significant business personal property (equipment, furniture, etc.), you'll likely owe property taxes to local jurisdictions.

Excise Tax

Certain industries face federal or state excise taxes on specific goods or activities, such as fuel, alcohol, tobacco or telecommunications services.

Ten Tax Planning Strategies to Maximize Savings

Now that you understand your obligations let's explore how to minimize them legally and ethically:

1. Choose the Right Business Structure

One of the most important tax decisions you'll make is selecting the appropriate entity structure. While many businesses start as sole proprietorships for simplicity, this may not be optimal as you grow.

S Corporations can be particularly advantageous for profitable service businesses, as they allow you to pay yourself a reasonable salary (subject to employment taxes) while taking additional profits as distributions (exempt from self-employment taxes). This strategy alone can save thousands in taxes annually.

C Corporations, while facing potential double taxation, may benefit companies that reinvest most profits into growth rather than distributing them to owners. They also offer more favorable treatment for certain fringe benefits and can utilize graduated tax rates for smaller corporations.

Case Study:
The Impact of Entity Selection

A professional services client generating $500,000 in annual profit saved over $15,000 in self-employment taxes by converting from an LLC to an S Corporation. By paying the owner a reasonable salary of $175,000 and taking the remaining $325,000 as distributions, they legally reduced their employment tax burden while maintaining full income tax compliance.

---

2. Maximize Business Deductions

The tax code allows businesses to deduct "ordinary and necessary" expenses, but many CEOs miss legitimate deductions simply because they don't properly track or categorize expenses. Implement these practices to capture all available deductions:

- **Implement expense tracking software** that integrates with your accounting system, making it easy to capture receipts and properly categorize expenses.
- **Create a tax-focused chart of accounts** that clearly separates deductible, partially deductible and non-deductible expenses.
- **Document the business purpose** for expenses that could be viewed as personal (meals, travel, entertainment) to support their deductibility.
- **Review fixed asset policies** to ensure you're optimizing depreciation strategies and taking advantage of immediate expensing options when available.

3. Leverage Retirement Plans

Qualified retirement plans offer powerful tax advantages for business owners:

Solo 401(k) plans allow self-employed individuals to contribute up to $23,500 (plus $7,500 catch-up if over 50) as employee contributions and approximately 25% of compensation as employer contributions, up to a combined maximum of $70,000 for 2025 ($77,500 if you are between 50 and 59, or older than 64. If you are between 60 and 63, the maximum is $81,250).

SEP IRAs permit employer contributions of up to 25% of compensation to a maximum of $70,000 (2025).

Defined benefit plans can allow for even larger contributions for older owners looking to accelerate retirement savings.

These contributions reduce your current taxable income while building tax-deferred retirement wealth. For businesses with employees, offering a 401(k) with employer matching can also create tax deductions while helping attract and retain talent.

4. Time Income and Expenses Strategically

With thoughtful planning, you can shift income and expenses between tax years to minimize your overall tax burden:

- **Defer income** into the next tax year by delaying billings or prepayments from customers in December if you anticipate being in a lower tax bracket next year.
- **Accelerate deductions** by making planned purchases before year-end, prepaying certain expenses (with careful attention to accounting rules) and maximizing fourth quarter estimated tax payments.
- **Consider tax rate arbitrage** between years, especially when tax law changes are anticipated.

5. Hire Family Members Strategically

Employing family members can create legitimate tax advantages:

- **Hiring your children** (if they're under 18 and your business is a sole proprietorship or partnership owned by parents) can shift income to their lower tax brackets while avoiding FICA taxes entirely. Ensure they perform actual work at market rates.

- **Employing your spouse** can enable additional retirement plan contributions and potentially create eligibility for certain fringe benefits.
- **Creating a family management company** can sometimes shift income and create deductions, though this requires careful structuring with professional guidance.

6. Implement Tax-Efficient Compensation Strategies

How you compensate yourself and key employees can significantly impact your tax situation:

- **Balance salary vs. distributions** for S corporation owners to minimize employment taxes while meeting "reasonable compensation" requirements.
- **Consider equity-based compensation** like stock options or restricted stock for key employees, which can create tax advantages for both the company and recipients.
- **Explore qualified fringe benefits** like health insurance, education assistance and dependent care assistance, which are typically deductible for the business but not taxable to employees.

7. Capture Research & Development Tax Credits

The R&D tax credit isn't just for large corporations or scientific research. If your company develops new products, processes, software, or formulas, you may qualify for this valuable dollar-for-dollar tax credit.

Activities that might qualify include:

Developing new or improved products or processes
Creating prototypes or models
Designing tools, jigs, molds, or dies
Developing or improving software
Conducting testing or certification

This credit can be particularly valuable for technology and manufacturing companies but is frequently overlooked.

8. Leverage Cost Segregation Studies

If your business owns commercial real estate, a cost segregation study can accelerate depreciation deductions by identifying components that can be depreciated over shorter lives (5, 7, or 15 years) rather than the standard 39 years for commercial property.

This strategy creates significant tax savings in the early years of property ownership through the time value of money, though it does require a professional engineering-based analysis.

9. Consider State and Local Tax Planning

While federal taxes often get the most attention, state and local taxes can significantly impact your bottom line:

- **Review nexus exposure** across states where you have employees, property, or significant sales to ensure compliance while minimizing obligations.
- **Explore incentive programs** offered by states and localities for business relocation, job creation, or capital investment.
- **Consider state tax consequences** when structuring operations, particularly for multi-state businesses that can optimize entity structure and intercompany transactions.

10. Develop a Tax-Efficient Exit Strategy

Even if selling your business seems far off, building tax efficiency into your exit planning can dramatically impact your after-tax proceeds:

- **Qualified Small Business Stock (QSBS)** exclusion can eliminate taxes on up to $10 million in gains when selling eligible C Corporation stock held for over five years.

- **Installment sales** can spread taxable gain over multiple years, potentially keeping you in lower tax brackets.
- **Tax-free reorganizations** may allow you to defer taxes when merging with or being acquired by another company in exchange for stock.
- **Estate planning techniques** like grantor retained annuity trusts (GRATs) or intentionally defective grantor trusts (IDGTs) can transfer business value to the next generation with minimal tax impact.

Working With Tax Professionals

While this chapter provides strategies to consider, effective tax planning requires qualified professional guidance. When selecting tax advisors:

- **Look beyond compliance** to find professionals who proactively recommend planning opportunities rather than just preparing returns.
- **Consider specialists** who understand your industry and business stage rather than generalists.
- **Establish a planning rhythm** with quarterly meetings focused on tax projections and planning opportunities, not just annual tax preparation.
- **Build a tax team** that includes both legal and accounting expertise for complex matters, ensuring your strategies are both legally sound and practically implementable.

Remember that the lowest-cost provider rarely delivers the best value when it comes to tax services. The right advisor will save you multiples of their fee through effective planning.

AI Tip

Leverage AI to identify potential tax deductions and optimization opportunities by analyzing your expense patterns and comparing them against tax code requirements. AI can spot deductions you might miss and ensure you're taking advantage of all available tax benefits throughout the year, not just at tax time.

Key Takeaways

- **Be proactive, not reactive**: Integrate tax planning into your year-round financial strategy rather than addressing it only during tax season.

- **Structure matters**: Your choice of business entity significantly impacts your tax obligations and should be periodically re-evaluated as your business evolves.

- **Documentation is critical**: Maintain robust records for business expenses, particularly those that could have personal elements, to support their deductibility.

- **Consider total tax burden**: Look beyond federal income tax to employment taxes, state obligations and potential exit taxes when making business decisions.

- **Leverage available incentives**: Research and development credits, cost segregation and retirement plans offer legitimate ways to reduce tax liability while building business value.

- **Invest in expertise**: The right tax professionals can identify opportunities you'd likely miss on your own, delivering value far exceeding their cost.

AI Key Takeaway Addition

Optimize tax strategies with AI analysis. AI can identify missed deductions and tax optimization opportunities by continuously analyzing expenses against current tax regulations.

Tip: The Benefit of Strategic Tax Planning

By approaching taxes strategically rather than viewing them as an inevitable burden, you can significantly increase your company's after-tax profits while ensuring compliance with increasingly complex regulations. The most successful business leaders recognize that effective tax planning isn't about aggressive schemes but rather about understanding the tax implications of business decisions and structuring operations to minimize obligations legally.

Strong financial operations and smart tax strategy put you in a position of strength. Now, you're ready to raise outside capital, but only if it's the right move for your business.

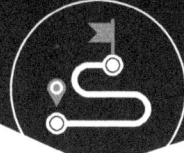

CHAPTER 11

Capital Raising Process

R aising capital is essential for growing businesses, yet many CEOs find this process intimidating and complex. For small business leaders, navigating the capital raising landscape can be as challenging as it is necessary. In this chapter, we'll explore the capital raising journey, its key steps and how to successfully secure the funding needed to take your business to the next level.

What is Capital Raising?

Capital raising is the process of securing funds to finance your business operations, fuel growth initiatives or manage cash flow challenges. While there are various sources of capital—from debt financing through loans to equity financing through investors—each comes with different implications for your business's ownership structure, control and financial obligations.

For small-business CEOs, understanding the fundamentals of capital raising is not merely about getting money; it's about finding the right partners who align with your vision, securing appropriate terms and ensuring the capital serves your specific business needs without creating undue burden. The right capital at the right time can accelerate your growth trajectory, while poorly structured financing can create constraints that limit your ability to execute your vision.

Why Raise Capital?

Before initiating a capital raise, it's essential to clarify your objectives. Common reasons small businesses seek external funding include growth financing, working capital needs, acquisition funding, research and development investments or debt refinancing.

Growth financing is perhaps the most common motivation, as expanding into new markets, launching new products, or scaling operations often requires significant investment beyond what your current cash flow can support. Similarly, managing day-to-day operations, especially during growth phases or seasonal fluctuations, sometimes necessitates additional working capital. Acquisition funding becomes relevant when purchasing another business or specific assets that require substantial capital not readily available from operations.

Research and development investments in new technologies, product improvements or innovations typically demand dedicated funding that may strain existing resources. Finally, debt refinancing can improve cash flow and reduce financial pressure by restructuring existing obligations on more favorable terms.

Beyond simply needing money, consider your reasons from an investor's perspective. Some motivations—like fueling proven growth strategies—will excite potential investors, while others, such as covering ongoing losses, might raise concerns. Being clear about your "why" helps ensure you approach the right funding sources with the right message.

The Capital Raising Roadmap

Successful capital raising follows a structured process that typically spans several months. Let's explore each step in detail.

1. Setting Goals (2–4 Weeks)

The first crucial step is clarifying what you want to accomplish and how your team will make it happen. This involves addressing key questions about your objectives, timeline and expectations.

Start by pinpointing why you want to raise capital beyond simply "needing money." Perhaps you're looking to improve your product by hiring more developers, increase production capacity to meet growing demand, or expand your customer base through enhanced marketing efforts. Being specific helps both you and potential investors understand the purpose and potential return on investment.

Next, determine how much capital you need and by when. This requires creating cash flow projections for the next three years to identify precisely how much funding you require and the timing of your needs. Without this clarity, you risk raising too little (forcing another round sooner than ideal) or too much (unnecessarily diluting ownership).

Consider what type of capital best suits your needs. Financial investors typically take a hands-off approach, providing capital while letting you run the business. Strategic investors, conversely, want to get involved, contributing resources or skills beyond funding. Each approach has merits depending on your specific situation and goals.

Honestly assess how much ownership you're willing to sacrifice. Determine the maximum equity stake you're comfortable offering and whether you're willing to give up majority control. This decision will significantly impact which funding sources are appropriate for your situation.

Finally, assign clear responsibilities to team members while ensuring your CEO remains front and center for pitches and key meetings. Capital raising can be all-consuming, so delegating effectively helps maintain business momentum during the process.

2. Financial Preparation & Assessment (4–5 Weeks)

This step involves substantial preparation and organization. For most companies, it requires significant cleanup and documentation assembly before approaching potential investors.

Begin by organizing your historical financials. Ensure your balance sheets, income statements and cash flow statements are accurate and comply with current accounting standards. Investors will scrutinize these documents to understand your business's financial health and trajectory.

Create a detailed financial model showing month-by-month projections of your current and anticipated cash positions for the next

three years. This model should incorporate your growth plans, allowing you to identify funding gaps and support your capital request with concrete numbers.

Acme Products, Inc.
Pro Forma Profit & Loss

	Month 1	Month 2	Month 3	Month 4	Month 5	Month 6	Month 7	Month 8
REVENUES								
eCommerce	4,643,470	4,643,470	4,643,470	4,643,470	4,643,470	4,643,470	4,643,470	4,643,470
Wholesale	1,100,403	1,100,403	1,100,403	1,100,403	1,100,403	1,100,403	1,100,403	1,100,403
Retail	266,000	266,000	266,000	266,000	381,500	381,500	381,500	381,500
BP Labs	0	0	0	0	0	0	0	0
BP Coaching	122,667	122,667	122,667	122,667	122,667	122,667	122,667	122,667
Shipping & Handling								
Total Revenues	**6,132,540**	**6,132,540**	**6,132,540**	**6,132,540**	**6,248,040**	**6,248,040**	**6,248,040**	**6,248,040**
COGS								
eCommerce & Wholesale								
Product Costs	2,412,427	2,412,427	2,412,427	2,412,427	2,412,427	2,412,427	2,412,427	2,412,427
Fulfillment Fee	114,877	114,877	114,877	114,877	114,877	114,877	114,877	114,877
Pickpak Fee	287,194	287,194	287,194	287,194	287,194	287,194	287,194	287,194
Shipping Expense	574,387	574,387	574,387	574,387	574,387	574,387	574,387	574,387
Supplier Management	0	0	0	0	0	0	0	0
Customer Service	14,360	14,360	14,360	14,360	14,360	14,360	14,360	14,360
Total eCommerce	3,403,245	3,403,245	3,403,245	3,403,245	3,403,245	3,403,245	3,403,245	3,403,245
Retail								
Product Costs	66,500	66,500	66,500	66,500	95,375	95,375	95,375	95,375
Total Retail	66,500	66,500	66,500	66,500	95,375	95,375	95,375	95,375
Total COGS	**3,469,745**	**3,469,745**	**3,469,745**	**3,469,745**	**3,498,620**	**3,498,620**	**3,498,620**	**3,498,620**
Gross Margin	**2,662,795**	**2,662,795**	**2,662,795**	**2,662,795**	**2,749,420**	**2,749,420**	**2,749,420**	**2,749,420**
	43.4%	43.4%	43.4%	43.4%	44.0%	44.0%	44.0%	44.0%
EXPENSES								
General & Administrative Expenses								
Payroll	250,583	256,217	256,217	256,217	256,217	372,217	256,217	256,217
Legal	50,000	50,000	50,000	50,000	50,000	50,000	50,000	50,000
Facilities	26,261	26,261	26,261	26,261	26,261	26,261	26,261	26,261
G&A (includes Ads)	20,500	20,500	20,500	20,500	20,500	20,500	20,500	20,500
Travel	20,333	20,333	20,333	20,333	20,333	20,333	20,333	20,333
Other Expense	72,300	72,300	72,300	72,300	72,300	72,300	72,300	72,300
Total General & Admin. Expenses	**439,977**	**445,611**	**445,611**	**445,611**	**445,611**	**561,611**	**445,611**	**445,611**
Product Development								
Direct R&D	28,000	129,500	28,000	32,500	28,000	99,500	48,000	48,000
Market Research	0	150,000	3,500	200,000	103,500	0	0	100,000
Payroll	93,269	93,269	93,269	93,269	93,269	93,269	93,269	93,269
Professional Fees	34,823	71,410	59,699	37,760	26,056	46,505	20,750	40,750
Other Expenses	45,050	50,050	46,900	45,750	45,750	50,500	47,700	47,800
Total Product Development	**201,142**	**494,229**	**231,367**	**409,278**	**296,575**	**289,773**	**209,719**	**329,819**
Marketing & Customer Service								
Payroll	264,302	264,302	264,302	264,302	264,302	264,302	264,302	264,302
Online Advertising	333,333	333,333	333,333	333,333	333,333	333,333	333,333	333,333
PR and Related Expense	83,900	95,400	97,900	100,400	116,589	128,433	134,544	137,387
Trade Shows / Product Demos / Other	107,198	107,198	107,198	107,198	107,198	107,198	107,198	107,198
Affiliate Commission	37,545	39,798	42,186	44,717	47,400	50,244	53,258	56,454
Product Demos	25,500	25,500	25,500	25,500	25,500	25,500	25,500	25,500
TV / Media / Podcasts	13,950	17,450	27,450	27,450	27,450	22,450	17,450	17,450
Contractors and Ambassadors	33,000	33,000	33,000	33,000	33,000	33,000	33,000	33,000
Other Expense	243,484	241,984	241,984	241,984	241,984	241,984	241,984	241,984
Total Marketing	**1,142,212**	**1,157,964**	**1,172,852**	**1,177,683**	**1,196,755**	**1,206,444**	**1,210,569**	**1,216,607**
Sales								
Payroll	147,391	147,391	147,391	147,391	147,391	147,391	147,391	147,391
Sales Commissions	39,000	44,000	44,000	49,000	49,000	49,000	49,000	49,000
Product Demo	5,000	5,000	5,000	5,000	5,000	5,000	5,000	5,000
Travel	30,000	30,000	30,000	30,000	30,000	30,000	30,000	30,000
Trade Shows	13,333	13,333	13,333	13,333	13,333	13,333	13,333	13,333
Other Expense	212,285	212,285	213,785	213,785	213,785	213,785	213,785	213,785
Total Sales	**447,009**	**452,009**	**453,509**	**458,509**	**458,509**	**458,509**	**458,509**	**458,509**

Retail Operations								
General & Admin (Direct)	17,325	17,325	17,325	17,325	17,325	17,325	17,325	17,325
Marketing	23,100	23,100	23,100	23,100	23,100	23,100	23,100	23,100
Other	17,325	17,325	17,325	17,325	17,325	17,325	17,325	17,325
Payroll Expense	67,667	67,667	67,667	67,667	101,500	101,500	101,500	101,500
Rent	15,000	15,000	15,000	15,000	22,500	22,500	22,500	22,500
Supplies	4,620	4,620	4,620	4,620	4,620	4,620	4,620	4,620
Utilities	4,620	4,620	4,620	4,620	4,620	4,620	4,620	4,620
Waste/Spoilage	4,620	4,620	4,620	4,620	4,620	4,620	4,620	4,620
Total Retail Operations	**154,277**	**154,277**	**154,277**	**154,277**	**195,610**	**195,610**	**195,610**	**195,610**
Bulletproof Training Institute								
Payroll Expense	28,520	28,520	28,520	28,520	28,520	28,520	28,520	28,520
Facilities	15,000	15,000	15,000	15,000	15,000	15,000	15,000	15,000
General & Administrative (Direct)	18,050	18,050	18,050	18,050	18,050	22,050	18,050	18,050
Other Expense	20,000	20,000	20,000	20,000	20,000	20,000	20,000	20,000
Total BTI	**81,570**	**81,570**	**81,570**	**81,570**	**81,570**	**85,570**	**81,570**	**81,570**
Total Expenses	**2,466,186**	**2,785,659**	**2,539,186**	**2,727,128**	**2,874,629**	**2,797,517**	**2,601,587**	**2,727,725**
Net Operating Income	**196,609**	-122,864	**123,609**	-64,333	**74,790**	-48,097	**147,833**	**21,695**
	3%	2%	2%	-1%	1%	-1%	2%	0%
Other Income								
Other Income	3,500	3,500	3,500	3,500	3,500	3,500	3,500	3,500
Total Other Income	**3,500**	**3,500**	**3,500**	**3,500**	**3,500**	**3,500**	**3,500**	**3,500**
Other Expenses								
Interest Expense								
Depreciation	117,200	118,052	118,904	119,756	120,623	121,491	122,359	123,227
Corp. Income Taxes	0	32,164	-95,967	2,282	-73,245	-17,933	-67,435	10,589
Currency Translation	0	0	0	0	0	0	0	0
Bad Debt Expense	2,500	2,500	2,500	2,500	2,500	2,500	2,500	2,500
Total Other Expenses	**119,700**	**152,716**	**25,437**	**124,538**	**49,888**	**106,058**	**57,424**	**136,316**
Net Other Income	-116,200	-149,216	-21,937	-121,038	-46,388	-102,558	-53,924	-132,816
After-Tax Net Income	**80,409**	-272,080	**101,672**	-185,371	**28,402**	-150,655	**93,909**	-111,122
EBITDA	**224,609**	**6,636**	**151,609**	-31,833	**102,790**	**51,403**	**195,833**	**69,695**

Sample Financial Model

Prepare a use of funds schedule documenting how you'll apply the capital you're seeking to grow your business. Investors expect specificity about where their money will go and what milestones it will help you achieve.

Update your capitalization table to clearly show current ownership stakes, ensuring all shareholder agreements are signed and organized. Many businesses lack proper documentation in this area, so addressing gaps now prevents complications during due diligence.

Refresh your business plan to create a comprehensive document showing your intentions for the next three years. This should include your mission, company description, market assessment, strategic objectives and implementation plans. While you won't share the full plan during initial meetings, having it ready supports your pitch and prepares you for detailed discussions.

Clarify acceptable funding terms by documenting what you're willing to accept or reject. This ensures alignment with your team before negotiations begin and helps you evaluate offers efficiently.

Finally, develop an initial investor list identifying targets who align with your goals. Track these prospects in a spreadsheet or CRM system to maintain organization as your outreach expands.

HISTORIC FINANCIALS
- Balance sheets
- Income statements
- Cash flow statements
- Accuracy & compliance check

FINANCIAL MODEL
- Current & expected revenue
- Current & expected expenses
- Month-by-month projections

SCHEDULE FOR USE OF FUNDS
- Sources of funds
- Planned expenses
- Summary document

CAP TABLE
- Collect signed agreements
- Summary document

BUSINESS PLAN
- Mission statement
- Company description
- Goals & objectives
- Market assessment
- Competitive assessment
- Product roadmap(s)
- Company structure
- Management bios
- Marketing / sales metrics

FUNDING DECISIONS
- Internal term sheet
- Team aligned

INVESTOR LIST
- List of target investors
- Tracking system (CRM)

Capital Raise Preparation Checklist

3. Materials Development & Due Diligence Preparation (5 Weeks)

This stage involves creating two sets of materials: marketing documents to attract investor interest and detailed information for due diligence once interest is established.

Marketing Materials

- Develop an **Executive Summary** or "**Teaser**" – a two-page professional document describing your company, vision and investment opportunity. You'll share this when requesting initial meetings, so it must be both informative and captivating.
- Develop an **Investor Pitch Deck** of 15–20 slides highlighting your vision, the problem you solve, your solution, market opportunity, business model, traction, team qualifications and funding needs. Keep text brief and focused on telling a compelling story rather than exhausting every detail.
- Create a **Press Kit** containing company information, team bios, awards and media coverage that investors can review after your presentation. This reinforces key points and provides additional context about your achievements and market recognition.

Due Diligence

- Prepare a comprehensive **Business Plan** detailing your business strategy, market position and growth plans. This document expands on your pitch deck with substantive analysis and implementation details.
- Refine your Detailed **Financial Model** to show revenue drivers, expenses and cash flow projections. This model should be robust enough to withstand scrutiny and scenario testing while clearly demonstrating your path to profitability or accelerated growth.
- Prepare a **Pro Forma Cap Table** showing ownership percentages after potential investment. This helps investors understand their potential stake and visualize the company's ownership structure post-investment.
- Gather **supporting documentation** including customer lists, contracts, intellectual property information and other relevant materials that substantiate your claims and address common investor questions.

4. Going to Market (4–6 Weeks)

With preparation complete, it's time to engage with potential investors through a strategic approach to meetings, pitches and negotiations.

Begin by practicing your pitch with advisors or existing investors to refine your messaging and prepare for tough questions. Presenting to investors differs significantly from other business presentations, so rehearsal is essential, even for experienced executives. Request candid feedback and adjust your approach accordingly.

Schedule initial meetings with target investors to introduce your company and gauge interest. Use your executive summary to secure these conversations, and keep initial discussions focused on establishing fit rather than diving into exhaustive details.

Deliver your pitch to interested parties, focusing on communicating your vision and opportunity. Remember that your goal is generating enough excitement for investors to request more information or additional meetings, not covering every aspect of your business plan.

Manage follow-up meetings with interested investors who want deeper information. These discussions typically explore specific aspects of your business model, market, financial projections, or team capabilities in greater detail.

Navigate negotiations by remaining flexible yet firm about your core requirements. Understand that investors will naturally challenge your assumptions and valuation to improve their terms. This process helps you identify investors who share your vision and can work constructively through disagreements.

Collect Letters of Intent (LOIs) from serious investors, which outline proposed terms. Your advisor or investment banker can help compare these offers and potentially leverage interest to improve terms across the board.

Select a lead investor whose reputation, terms and strategic alignment best fit your needs. Remember that the highest valuation isn't always the best choice if it comes with problematic terms or a partner who doesn't share your vision for the company.

5. Due Diligence and Closing the Deal (6–8 Weeks)

The final stage involves intensive scrutiny of your business as investors verify your claims and formalize the investment terms.

During this phase, investors look at your company under a microscope, examining the information behind your assertions and speaking with customers, suppliers, employees and other stakeholders. **Respond promptly to information requests and provide complete, accurate answers to maintain momentum and credibility.**

Work with experienced legal counsel to review and negotiate term sheets, shareholder agreements and other closing documents. Standard legal documents from the National Venture Capital Association can serve as starting points, helping control legal costs while ensuring appropriate protections for all parties.

Address concerns constructively as they arise during due diligence. Investors invariably discover things not fully disclosed or understood during initial discussions. How you handle these issues significantly impacts whether the deal proceeds and on what terms.

Sign final agreements, which may include shareholder agreements, stock purchase agreements and board resolutions. Depending on your company's structure and the investment specifics, closing documentation can range from relatively simple to quite extensive.

Finally, announce your funding to employees, customers and the broader market as appropriate. This communication should emphasize how the investment advances your mission and benefits your stakeholders, not just the dollar amount raised.

Key Fundraising Considerations

Valuation Methodologies

Understanding how investors value businesses can help you set realistic expectations and negotiate effectively. For established companies, investors typically use methodologies like Comparable Company Analysis (examining valuations of similar businesses), Discounted Cash Flow (calculating the present value of projected future cash flows), Market Multiple Method (applying industry-standard multiples to revenue or earnings) or Cost-to-Duplicate Approach (estimating the cost to build a similar business from scratch).

For early-stage companies without significant revenue, valuations often rely more on potential market size, intellectual property, team expertise and early traction. In these cases, valuation becomes as much art as science, with investors making judgment calls about your company's growth potential and likelihood of capturing market share.

Whatever valuation approach applies to your situation, prepare to defend your position with solid data and reasonable assumptions. Be particularly careful about claiming "unicorn status" prematurely, as unrealistic valuations can create future financing challenges even if initially successful.

Case Study:
The Danger in Overestimating Valuation

A Software-as-a-Service (SaaS) startup looking to do its first institutional capital raise once came to us for advice. The management team had no experience building SaaS companies, much less successfully completing a fundraising exercise with venture capital funds. The product was very technical but promising, because it applied to a wide variety of enterprise clients.

We helped them create a 5-year pro forma financial model that showed the typical "hockey stick" growth that all startups think they will be able to achieve once they have proper funding. The model was sound, but the assumptions (as provided by the founders) were not. In our experience, VCs only believe projections when the company can back them up with defensible data, ideally with a track record of successful sales growth. Unfortunately, this company lacked such data. Although this was precisely the coaching the management team had asked for, they refused to listen to our advice.

What made the situation worse was that the team believed they could get a valuation of more than $100 million when they had virtually no revenues. Companies in their same vertical had received funding at sky-high valuations, so they thought they could easily get the same terms.

After being turned down numerous times, they backed off their expectations considerably. But unfortunately, more than 12 months had gone by, and they still had no actual sales. So, they never obtained funding, and the company was in danger of closing its doors. In this case, the unsupported financial model was just one missing piece of the puzzle. The real issue was the hubris that led to the company's over-zealous approach to raising capital and ended up being their ultimate undoing.

Equity vs. Debt Financing

Both equity and debt have their place in a small business's capital structure, and understanding the tradeoffs helps you choose the right approach for your specific needs.

Equity financing offers several advantages: no repayment obligation, investors sharing risk and potential strategic partnerships that bring expertise beyond capital. However, it also dilutes your ownership, possibly reduces your control and creates investor expectations for significant returns that may influence your decision-making.

Debt financing allows you to maintain ownership while benefiting from tax-deductible interest and a predictable repayment schedule. On the downside, it requires regular payments regardless of profitability, may involve personal guarantees and often includes covenant restrictions that limit your operational flexibility.

Many businesses benefit from a balanced approach, using debt for assets that generate returns exceeding interest costs and using equity for higher-risk growth initiatives or when cash flow is insufficient to service additional debt. The right mix depends on your growth stage, industry dynamics, risk tolerance and available options.

Types of Investors

Different investors bring varying expectations, resources and engagement levels. Angel investors are typically high-net-worth individuals investing their own money in earlier stages. They may provide valuable mentorship but generally invest smaller amounts ($25K–$500K) and may have less structured processes than institutional investors.

Venture Capital firms are professional investment companies managing pooled funds, typically seeking high-growth opportunities with clear exit strategies. They usually invest in specific sectors, stages and deal sizes, focusing on companies that can potentially return their entire fund through a successful exit.

Private Equity firms focus on more established businesses, often seeking controlling stakes and implementing operational improvements to increase value. Their investment horizon is typically longer than venture capital, and they may bring significant operational expertise to portfolio companies.

Strategic investors are corporations investing in smaller companies for strategic reasons, such as access to new technologies, distribution channels or markets. Beyond capital, they can offer valuable industry connections and partnerships, though their strategic objectives may sometimes conflict with maximizing shareholder value.

Family Offices are private wealth management firms serving ultra-high-net-worth families, increasingly acting as direct investors with longer investment horizons than traditional VCs. They often have more flexible mandates and can be more patient capital, though their decision-making processes may be less predictable.

Understanding these different investor types helps you target your outreach to those most likely to be interested in your specific situation, saving time and increasing your chances of finding the right partner.

Fundraising Documentation

Professional documentation significantly impacts investor perception and streamlines the process. Your pitch deck should be a concise presentation (15–20 slides) highlighting your vision, problem, solution, market size, business model, traction, team and funding needs. Focus on clarity and compelling storytelling rather than exhaustive detail, as the goal is to generate enough interest for further conversation.

An executive summary is a 1–2-page document covering key aspects of the opportunity, functioning as an initial screening tool for potential investors. This document should be engaging enough to secure a meeting while providing sufficient information for investors to determine basic fit.

Your financial model provides a detailed projection of your business's financial performance, demonstrating your understanding of key drivers and providing a basis for valuation discussions. This should be sophisticated enough to allow scenario testing while remaining grounded in realistic assumptions.

Due diligence materials form a comprehensive collection of corporate, financial, legal and operational documents that substantiate your claims and address investor concerns. Having these organized in advance dramatically improves the efficiency of the due diligence process and demonstrates your professionalism and preparation. You will want to setup a "virtual data room" where all your corporate documents are stored so that an investor can efficiently review all of them in an organized manner.

Common Pitfalls to Avoid

Unrealistic Valuation Expectations

Setting an unreasonably high valuation may feel gratifying initially but can lead to significant problems. Investors may pass immediately, or worse, you might secure funding on terms that set unrealistic expectations for future rounds. This can lead to a problematic "down round" later, damaging both morale and market perception.

The solution is researching comparable companies in your space, consulting with advisors familiar with current market conditions and preparing to justify your valuation with solid metrics and milestones. Remember that a slightly lower valuation with the right partner often creates more long-term value than a higher number with problematic terms or partners.

Not Raising Enough Capital

Many founders underestimate the time and capital required to achieve meaningful milestones. Raising too little may force you to begin another fundraising process before achieving substantial progress, putting you in a weaker negotiating position and creating a negative perception of your planning abilities.

To avoid this, calculate how much capital you need to reach the next significant value-creating milestone, then add a 25–50% buffer for unexpected challenges and opportunities. While this approach may mean accepting more dilution initially, it typically results in better long-term outcomes by providing sufficient runway to demonstrate material progress.

Neglecting Investor Fit

Not all money is equal. Investors bring different expectations, time horizons, expertise and networks. The wrong investor relationship can create significant friction and distract from building your business, particularly when strategic disagreements arise or when your timeline doesn't align with theirs.

Research potential investors thoroughly, including speaking with founders they've previously backed. Seek investors who understand your industry, share your vision for the company's future and can contribute beyond capital. A slightly lower valuation from the right partner typically creates more value than optimal terms with a misaligned investor.

Losing Focus on the Business

Fundraising demands significant time and attention from company leadership; therefore, it can distract founders, hurting business performance and investor appeal. To stay balanced, set dedicated fundraising time, delegate operations and consider a fractional CFO.

Remember that the strongest negotiating position comes from demonstrating that your business continues to thrive regardless of the fundraising outcome.

AI Tip

Use AI-powered financial modeling tools to create dynamic investor presentations that can instantly show different scenarios and assumptions. This capability allows you to respond to investor questions in real-time with updated projections, demonstrating sophistication and preparedness that builds confidence.

Key Takeaways

- **Start with a clear plan.** Define why you need capital, how much you need and what you're willing to give up. A well-defined strategy helps you target the right investors.

- **Preparation is key.** Organize your financials, refine your pitch materials and ensure your business plan is investor-ready. Strong preparation builds confidence and credibility.

- **Choose investors wisely.** Look for partners who offer more than money—experience, industry insights and strategic value can be just as important as funding.

- **Stay structured and proactive.** Manage investor outreach and due diligence efficiently to avoid fundraising becoming a drain on your time and resources.

- **Build a resilient business.** Your company should be strong enough to succeed with or without outside funding. A solid foundation gives you better leverage in negotiations.

AI Key Takeaway Addition

Enhance investor presentations with AI-powered modeling. Dynamic financial models that update in real-time demonstrate sophistication and enable immediate response to investor scenario questions.

Once you begin fundraising, understanding the investor's mindset becomes critical. Let's explore what investors really want and how to speak their language.

CHAPTER 12

What Investors Really Want

Understanding Investor Perspective

At some point, nearly every entrepreneur considers finding a strategic partner or selling to an investor who can take their business to the next level. Whether this was your plan all along or a reaction to unexpected news, it probably got you thinking—how much could your company be worth?

Business valuation is a complex process, but that doesn't mean you can't influence the outcome. Quite the opposite, in fact. What you do today can dramatically alter your company's future market value.

I have talked with founders who thought they could get 8x–10x earnings for their company (as reflected by EBITDA), only to receive offers 25%–50% below that range. They were shocked. Sometimes, that price was a reflection of the overall market and variables beyond their control. However, it is often the case that better planning and targeted investments in a company's infrastructure and operations can result in a significantly higher valuation.

To make your company attractive to investors, you must step into the buyers' shoes and ask the question that's foremost in their mind: *"What's in it for me?"* Only then can you evaluate your business through an investor's lens and make meaningful changes.

How Investors Determine Business Valuation

When pressed to explain the valuation process, investors will tell you that they look at a myriad of both qualitative and quantitative measures. Each investor will have their own approach which will differ based on their experience, industry, investment philosophy, capital structure and more. However, virtually all investors/buyers will look closely at certain financial KPIs that demonstrate a company's current or anticipated revenue growth or profitability, then apply a multiple.

Profitability KPIs, like EBITDA, are primarily a measure of where your company is today. But the KPIs that investors will utilize in their financial models can vary, depending on the business. For instance, investors often assess middle-market companies (~$15 million in revenue or more) based on EBITDA. Whereas with smaller businesses (early-stage growth), investors may look at revenue instead.

The multiple, however, reflects a wide variety of factors, each of which indicates whether your organization is in a strong position to achieve growth. After all, investors are not looking for companies that have already reached their full potential. They want opportunities where they can take a business to the next level and get a return on their investment.

Where this gets tricky is that every industry is different; expectations vary depending on your stage of growth. In SaaS, for instance, it's relatively easy to arrive at a valuation because there are common, industry-published multiples that investors can use. As long as you have a well-constructed KPI dashboard with common KPIs like ARR (annual recurring revenue), MRR (monthly recurring revenue), bookings, LTV (lifetime value of a customer) and churn, investors can indicate a recommended range. Then they examine other factors (such as the uniqueness of the product, stage of growth, etc.) to determine whether the multiple should be on the higher or lower end of that range.

There are other industries, however, where it is much less clear. In the entertainment industry, for example, success can vary based on whether your production was a hit. In this case, profitability trends simply aren't reliable, and intangibles such as branding or celebrity status can influence results.

There can also be circumstances where a company has no profitability KPIs at all. A biotech firm, for instance, might operate at a loss as it develops cutting-edge, life-saving technologies and jumps through the necessary regulatory hoops. Yet its growth, addressable market and revenue potential could be enormous, which would put it in a position to command billions of dollars.

Therefore, to arrive at an appropriate multiple, investors look at three areas of your business: your financials, the health of your company and your growth potential, while keeping the following key questions in mind:

1. Has this company been generating revenue and profit? If so, how?
2. What are the risks? In other words, what will prevent me from replicating their success?
3. What is unique about this company?
4. What makes this a better deal than building it from scratch? How will this empower me to drive growth?

Let's explore each area in detail and offer suggestions for how you might improve the value of your company.

Strong Financials

As mentioned, investors look for companies that are poised for growth. So, one of the first areas they will review is your financials.

It is important to realize that they will look well beyond your standard income statements and balance sheets. One of the key things investors want to know is not just if you've been generating revenue and profit, but how. This will help them determine whether they can replicate (and build upon) your success.

In addition to financial statements, investors want to see strong financial processes and controls—things that indicate that you know exactly what's working, what isn't and what to do about it. Fortunately, these things are necessary for any healthy, growing company (whether you're looking for investors or not).

So, what steps can you take to shore up your finances?

- **Make sure you have a well-maintained set of books and financial statements** that are overseen by a financially savvy person. Although you may have a fantastic bookkeeper, consider hiring a controller or even a CFO who can audit your historical information to confirm that it's reliable and compliant.

- **If you haven't already, get an appropriate accounting system in place**—one that can tie into other systems, like an ERP solution. This will improve the reliability of your data and help ensure that things don't slip through the cracks.
- **Perform a reconciliation of cash and develop a detailed, realistic cash flow forecast**. A cash flow forecast starts with your cash position today and projects forward based on your anticipated revenues and expenses. It provides deep visibility into how you are generating and spending money and where things will stand each month. Ideally, it will also allow you to test scenarios so you can anticipate shortfalls.
- **Make sure you have an effective system in place for accounts payables and receivables** that adheres to best practices. You'd be surprised how many companies develop cash flow issues because they fail to collect what they're owed in a timely manner (i.e. 30–45 days) or pay their own vendors too quickly (i.e., right away instead of establishing a pattern of 30+ days after invoice).
- **Develop a KPI dashboard, comprehensive monthly management reports and commit to a monthly review process** with your executive team. This will empower you to spot and address problems quickly before they spin out of control.

Company Health

The second aspect of your company investors will explore is the overall health of the business. The goal here is to unearth the answer to their next big question: *What are the risks?*

In other words, if I peel back the elements that support this company's ability to generate revenue and profit, what will inhibit my ability to replicate that success? In this case, investors will focus on the following three areas.

Management

It is well known that success or failure in business is all about management, but what investors look for here will greatly depend on the type of business you have and what will happen after the transition.

For example, if you have been building a middle-market company that serves a national or even global market, you will need a well-structured management team. And, ideally, at least some of those people will stay with the company after the transaction. It is not easy to hire, structure, incentivize and train a strong, reputable management team. So even if there are problems with your company, buyers will often pay a premium if your management team is top-notch.

So, what should you do?

- **Backfill Yourself.** Many times, the founder/CEO is the only person who has built key customer and supplier relationships, and is often the best salesperson on the team. You need to be able to remove yourself from the day-to-day running of the business, be it sales, operations, or finance. Make sure your team can run the business without you. Could you take a 3-month vacation and not miss a beat? That's your goal!

- **Start Laying the Framework for a Smooth Transition**. If important, "indispensable" people could potentially leave the business at the time of an exit, investors would see this as a major risk. Take steps to mitigate this risk now. Identify and train successors and transfer key relationships and responsibilities to them at least 6 months before looking for potential buyers. Finally, think about retention plans/bonus structures post-transition.

- **Document Your Goals and Strategies, Then Develop a Communication Plan**. Investors will speak to people throughout the company (not just your management team) in search of weak links and disconnects, so you will want to ensure that each person can, and will, deliver a consistent message.

- **Examine Your Management Team Through the Investor's Eyes**. When firms are getting started, it is common to fill critical roles with friends and family, regardless of their credentials. To an investor, this can be a red flag. You must be able to justify these hires or consider making adjustments.

Customers

In a perfect world, your business will have a broad mix of loyal customers who deliver a reliable source of revenue and cash flow. But in the real world, most businesses will have some problems in this area. Investors expect this, so the key here is to show a strong grasp of where your strengths and weaknesses lie and to have a plan for addressing vulnerabilities.

- **Balance (or Rebalance) Your Customer Mix.** As we mentioned above, it is best to have a diverse mix of customers. If 80% of your business comes from just 20% of your customers, investors will see this as a warning sign (formally, "customer concentration risk"), so it is important to develop a plan for addressing imbalances. There are cases, however, where an imbalance can make sense. For instance, if you run a financial services company, you might have some extremely wealthy customers who have been with your company for years or who you are uniquely qualified to serve, justifying the risk.
- **Turn a Keen Eye to Your Pricing Model.** How vulnerable is your business to the whims of the market? Some volatility is normal, but if your pricing shifts with the economy, you must be able to show potential investors how this affects your margins and cash flow, plus how you weather the inevitable ups and downs.
- **Improve the Stickiness of Your Products or Services.** Is it easy for your customers to switch to another provider or go without your products and services? If so, what do you do to ensure a steady revenue stream? Again, this will be highly dependent on your industry. If, for example, you have a wholesale manufacturing business, you can increase "stickiness" by providing superior customer service.
- **Showcase Your Reputation.** In today's competitive market, your reputation speaks volumes about your company's longevity. You need customer-sanctioned case studies (B2B) or glowing reviews (B2C) that speak to the results you've delivered. If you are lacking in this area, pull together a team to address it.

Infrastructure

Every company must have an infrastructure in place for the business to run smoothly, the precise components of which will vary. You need to ensure that you have the proper people, processes, systems, policies, procedures, data and reporting that will enable a buyer to easily scale the business. For example, if a buyer brings you enough new customers to double revenue, can your back office handle the lift?

Savvy investors will sniff out any vulnerabilities in your infrastructure, especially those that could affect your cash flow, which (in turn) will inhibit their ability to replicate your success. Therefore, it is important to review the infrastructure of your business before engaging with investors so you can identify and address your weaknesses.

You will need to customize the following list based on the nature of your business, but as ideas:

- **Identify and Address Risk in Your Supply Chain**. What products or services do you rely upon to run your business? What would happen if any part of this breaks down? If, for example, you run a dry-cleaning business and you must pay your suppliers up-front for the chemicals required to fill customer orders, you must be able to explain to an investor how you ensure that you have enough cash on hand. And what happens if your supplier fails to deliver? Do you have another source you can count on? Who owns that relationship?

- **Develop a Backup Plan for Your Equipment & Facilities**. Do you own or lease the facilities you need to run your business? If you lease, what are the terms? If you rent a building and the lease is up at the end of the year, how can you assure a potential investor of your longevity? Will you still be capable of running your business if your landlord refuses to renew the lease?

- **Build Systems, Processes & Controls**. What policies and procedures do you have in place to ensure that you have the right people on your team, that your expectations are clear and to avoid fraud or compliance violations? For example: What does your hiring process look like? Can you quickly find and onboard the people you need to run your business? Do you have a financial infrastructure in place? Can your accounting system scale as you grow? Have you developed expense reimbursement, travel and entertainment policies? Do you have a process for sales forecasting? If not, what are your plans for developing these initiatives?

Growth Potential

Once they have a firm grip on where your company stands today, investors will shift their focus to factors that demonstrate growth potential. This is where things get exciting, because investors are looking to understand what is unique about your company. In other words, investors want to know if it would be smarter to invest in your business than in a competing firm or in a new venture.

By stepping into the investor's shoes and looking at your organization through their eyes, you have an opportunity to get ahead of this. You may notice things about your company that could really shine with a little extra effort. Or you may find ways to position yourself as a good fit for certain types of investors. On the flip side, of course, you may find problems. But it's better to catch and deal with them now before you find yourself in the midst of a sale.

One of our CFOs told me a story about working with a company that bought data centers. As it entered negotiations with potential acquirers, it learned that while the company was healthy and in a strong financial position, its data centers were so full that there was limited growth potential—and the deal fell through. If the company had gotten ahead of this and moved some resources around to allow for expansion space, they might have avoided this situation.

To that end, we'd like you to focus on your products and services, along with your marketing activities.

Products & Services

The fundamental goal of any business should be addressing the needs of its customers and solving their problems better than anyone else. Furthermore, companies that provide discretionary (nice-to-have) products or services are going to have a much more difficult time getting and retaining customers. So, investors look for companies with teams that have a deep understanding of and compassion for their customers and who strive to make their products and services indispensable.

Teams of this nature have initiative and purpose. They're disciplined and focused with their approach to adding value. This makes it much easier for an investor to step in, contribute to their mission and get a return on their investment.

So, what can you do to illuminate the value of your solutions?

- **Revisit Your Product Roadmap**. Where are you at in terms of development? Will accelerating certain plans make your offer more valuable? Are there things you can add that will help you break into new markets or modifications you could suggest that would allow you to solve a more pressing problem? Anything that would make your solutions more complete or satisfying is worth exploring.
- **Examine Your Product Mix**. Is there something special about your offer that makes it a particularly good bet for investors? For example, if your customers sign long-term contracts and you have a sizable base of clients, this will indicate that your cash flow is strong and predictable. With this as a foundation, investors would be free to focus on growth. Another possibility is to increase your profit margins by reducing the cost of your products or services, or by adding complementary offerings to your product mix to boost top-line revenue. Remember, investors seek opportunities where they can scale the business while earning a high ROI.
- **Clarify Your Unique Selling Proposition**. How do you stand out against your competition? Do you offer something unique? If not, what is your angle? Perhaps you deliver more value for a lower cost, or maybe you position yourself as a premium brand that is more suitable to certain, quality-minded clients. There is no "right" answer here, but this is an important thing for any organization to define, not only those seeking investors.

Marketing

You have developed an amazing product or service to address the needs of your customers, but how are you bringing those customers in the door? Investors will want to know that you've thought about this, deeply. You must be able to explain who your target audience is, where you can find them and what you have already done (or intend to do) to catch their attention and convert them into paying customers.

Once again, much of this will depend on your industry, but here are a few things you can do that are common for many types of businesses:

- **Reexamine Your Total Addressable Market (TAM) Assumptions**. Since you know investors like to see an opportunity for growth, think about possibilities from their viewpoint. For instance, if you have a small company with a niche product, you may have limited your scope to a certain geographical location due to distribution constraints. If you can attract an investor with a strong distribution network, your total addressable market may be much larger.
- **Assess the Competitive Landscape and Your Positioning**. What's special about how you have positioned yourself in the market?
  - Do you have a large market share?
  - Have you built a strong brand and reputation when compared to your competitors?
  - Have you developed a website with quality content that performs well in search and on social media—attracting traffic, leads and sales?
  - How is your product priced compared to the competition? Is there an opportunity to raise prices?

  A company's positioning doesn't happen overnight. It is the result of careful planning and execution. Therefore, any accomplishments add to the value of your company. So, it is important to clarify what you've done and where the opportunities lie.

- **Evaluate Your Partnerships and Channels**. Some companies have strong marketing or referral partners who are a reliable source of leads. If this is the situation for you, examine those relationships to determine what would happen in the event of a change of ownership. Are those connections dependent on a certain person staying with the company? If so, are there steps you can take to make them more durable? Or do you see opportunities for developing new partnerships with the help of a strategic investor? Secondly, examine your channel mix for any quick wins. There may be easy opportunities to improve your cost of acquisition—a KPI investors are sure to look at.

- **Document the Barriers to Entry**. When you are building a company, you don't always stop to take inventory of the challenges you encounter along the way. When you are considering a sale, however, it is important to highlight them. Document each significant roadblock you have already overcome because each one adds to your company's value. Perhaps there were industry regulations to adhere to, licensing issues to overcome, or geographical constraints to work around. What tasks are complete and what could fuel your growth?

- **Capture Your Marketing Plans in Writing**. This may sound obvious, but if you've been busy building your business and haven't taken the time to document your marketing plans, don't worry—your secret is safe with us. However, before you engage with investors, it is important to take all of those brilliant plans in your head and capture them in writing. We promise it will be worth your while. Documenting your plans may seem tedious, but such records are crucial for communicating your value to investors and for coordinating with team members.

AI Tip

Implement AI analytics to create detailed customer profitability and predictive models that show investors exactly which segments drive value and growth potential. This level of insight demonstrates the data-driven decision-making and scalability that sophisticated investors seek.

Key Takeaways

- **Think like an investor.** Assess your company through their lens to uncover opportunities to increase its value.

- **Answer the big questions.** Investors care about ROI and growth potential; demonstrate how your business delivers both.

- **Get ahead of potential issues.** Conduct a pre-diligence check to identify and fix red flags before approaching investors.

- **Strengthen your financial foundation.** Solid reporting, controls and visibility make your company more attractive to investors.

- **Position for long-term success.** Investors want scalable businesses; showcase a strong team, resilient operations and a clear growth strategy.

AI Key Takeaway Addition

Showcase AI-driven insights to investors. Demonstrating advanced analytics capabilities and data-driven decision-making signals operational sophistication that investors value in scalable businesses.

Tip: The BIG Questions on EVERY Investor's Mind

Before seeking investors, evaluate your business from their perspective. A pre-diligence check helps identify and address potential issues, strengthening your company's position.

Investors focus on two key questions: **"What's in it for me?"** *and* **"How can I grow this company for a return?"**

Understanding their evaluation criteria allows you to enhance your business's value and marketability.

With a clear view of what investors want, you're in a better position to scale or prepare for an eventual exit. Let's wrap up by reviewing how to put all the pieces together for long-term success.

PART 4

The Final Stretch

CHAPTER 13

Conclusion

I n the early stages of a company, CEOs get involved in *everything*. However, as your growth ramps up, you must become strategic with your time. You need to put systems in place for building and scaling a financially viable business while preserving your attention for mission-critical items.

As a fractional CFO for growth companies, I help clients navigate this shift daily. I've found the following tips useful in nearly every situation.

Tip 1: Develop Relationships with Strategic Partners

Every business leader understands they need a strategy for attracting and converting new leads into customers. But you must be creative when growing sales on a budget. Instead of costly ad campaigns or branding strategies, I recommend you build strong, reciprocal partnerships first and do so as soon as possible.

I am not referring to simple networking. I'm talking about identifying companies with business models that complement your own and approaching them with a win-win proposition. The relationship can be formal or informal, but the key is to offer something valuable in exchange for inexpensive exposure to your target audience.

For example, when I founded my software company, Xtiva, we employed this strategy from the start. We had developed a back-office solution tailored to the unique needs of financial services firms. We approached a well-established company that provided services to brokerage firms and proposed that we form a marketing alliance. We offered their clients preferred pricing and services in exchange for marketing and sales support.

Our partner acquired a value-add for their customers, and we gained a customer base for little cost.

Tip 2: Build a Scalable Financial Infrastructure

When starting out, most small companies can get by with a simple book-keeping service. As the business grows, however, you will quickly require a more sophisticated financial infrastructure that can evolve as you scale. For instance, a growing business should have:

- An accounting solution that meets your business requirements.
- A detailed and realistic financial model where you can visualize your monthly income, expenses and cash flow projections for the coming year.
- A key performance indicators (KPI) dashboard.
- Basic internal controls, such as policies and procedures for accounts payable, accounts receivable and expense reimbursements.

That will help you spot problems and deal with them before they spin out of control while providing your executive team with the insight it needs to make financially sound business decisions.

Tip 3: Grow Your Team Slowly by Including Contractors in Your Hiring Plans

You need a team of smart, reliable people to help you pursue your goals. But hiring is expensive. Besides a full-time salary, employees expect benefits, bonuses, vacation time and equipment. Furthermore, you will need recruitment support and help building and managing your compensation plans. Although some of this is unavoidable, you can minimize your financial burden by including contractors in your hiring plans.

For example, instead of hiring a full-time marketing director and expecting them to be a jack-of-all-trades, consider hiring a team of freelancers. That will provide you with the expertise you need without the headcount. The same approach can apply to your management team. A fully burdened CFO can cost between $300,000 and $400,000 annually (sometimes more for "hot" areas like software as a service) and might be more than you need. Hiring a fractional CFO to provide advice and guidance is a more cost-effective option.

Tip 4: Prepare Yourself (and Your Business) for the Inevitable Pursuit of Capital

There often comes a time when companies need to raise some form of capital, and it will probably happen sooner than you think—especially if you are focused on growth. While you are likely to bring someone on board to help with this process, there are some things you can do now to prepare. Setting up your financial infrastructure, as we discussed earlier, is a great start. But it would also be beneficial to:

Familiarize yourself with the various sources of capital

When the time comes, you will need to decide what type of capital is right for you, but the options can be dizzying. Will you be looking for a simple debt arrangement? A strategic partner? A hands-off investor? And what would you be willing to give up in return? Exploring your options ahead of time can help you get comfortable with the lingo and tradeoffs so that the choices won't be so overwhelming.

Formalize your business and marketing plans

Any reputable lender or investor will expect to see your plans for running and monetizing your business. If none of your plans are in writing, or if they only exist on the back of cocktail napkins, consider drafting something more formal before starting down the capital-raising path.

Tip 5: Maintain Focus on Growing the Value of Your Business

Remember, although you are in growth mode, your primary role as a CEO remains the same. You must keep your company on track toward achieving its vision. That means you need to focus on ensuring that you have:

- A reputable product or service that solves a real problem for real customers.
- Traction with a diverse or defensible mix of customers (i.e., a reliable client base you can nurture and grow).
- A strong and trustworthy management team to whom you can delegate.
- A plan for increasing your company's value over the next 5-plus years.

As the CEO, your job is to get your company into a strong position so you can pursue whatever opportunities arise. Whether you believe you will eventually go public or decide to sell, it doesn't matter. Protect yourself from distractions so you can effectively grow and improve the value of your business.

The Bottom Line

When companies shift into growth mode, it's an adjustment for everyone, including the CEO. Therefore, it can be helpful to narrow the focus. Choose strategies that allow you to prepare for and pursue opportunities while continuing to minimize costs and reduce risks. This practice will allow you to build a thriving business.

AI Tip

As you scale your business, use AI as a force multiplier for your strategic initiatives. Whether it's identifying the most profitable partnerships, optimizing pricing strategies, or predicting market opportunities, AI can accelerate your ability to execute on growth plans while maintaining operational efficiency.

CHAPTER 14

AI in Finance: Accelerating Growth and Profitability [1]

A s a CEO, you're constantly looking for ways to grow faster, operate more efficiently and stay ahead of the competition. Artificial Intelligence (AI) has moved beyond the realm of tech giants and is now accessible to businesses of all sizes—including yours. The question isn't whether AI will impact your industry, but how quickly you can leverage it to gain a competitive advantage.

This chapter isn't about the technical aspects of AI or machine learning algorithms. Instead, it focuses on practical applications that can directly impact your bottom line, accelerate decision-making and help you scale more efficiently. Think of AI as another tool in your growth toolkit—one that can handle routine tasks while freeing your team to focus on strategic initiatives that drive value.

Why CEOs Should Care About AI in Finance

Many business leaders still view AI as futuristic technology that's either too expensive or too complex for their operations. This perception is outdated and costly. Today's AI tools are designed for practical business applications, often requiring minimal technical expertise to implement and delivering measurable returns within months.

Consider this: while you're manually analyzing last month's financial performance, your AI-enabled competitor is already adjusting pricing,

---

[1] Written by Claude.AI

identifying at-risk customers and optimizing cash flow for next quarter. The businesses that adopt AI early will have significant advantages in speed, accuracy and insight over those that wait.

Case Study: The Manufacturing CEO Who Gained 15 Days

A manufacturing client with $8 million in revenue was spending two weeks each month closing their books. Their controller and accountant worked overtime reconciling accounts, categorizing expenses and preparing reports. By implementing AI-powered automation tools, they reduced their month-end close to three days—giving the CEO financial insights 11 days sooner than before.

More importantly, the freed-up time allowed their finance team to focus on forward-looking analysis instead of historical data entry. The CEO now receives weekly cash flow projections and monthly profitability analysis by customer segment—insights that helped them identify their most profitable product lines and adjust their sales strategy accordingly.

Faster, Better Business Decisions

The speed of decision-making often determines whether you capture opportunities or watch competitors seize them. Traditional financial reporting provides a rearview mirror perspective—telling you what happened weeks after it occurred. AI transforms this dynamic by providing real-time insights and predictive analytics that help you stay ahead of trends.

Instead of waiting until month-end to understand your financial position, AI can provide daily updates on key metrics. You'll know immediately when cash flow is trending below projections, when a major customer's payment pattern changes, when product margins shift due to cost fluctuations, or when revenue concentration becomes risky. This real-time visibility enables proactive management rather than reactive problem-solving. You can address issues while they're manageable instead of discovering them when options are limited.

Cash flow surprises can derail growth plans or force difficult decisions about payroll and vendor payments. AI analyzes your historical payment patterns, seasonal trends and current pipeline to predict cash positions 30-90 days in advance with remarkable accuracy. For example, AI can identify that your largest customer typically pays 15 days later during their fiscal year-end quarter, allowing you to plan accordingly. Or it might detect that certain product lines have longer collection cycles, helping you adjust payment terms or customer targeting.

Beyond prediction, AI never sleeps, never takes vacation and never misses important changes in your business metrics. You can set up intelligent alerts that notify you when monthly recurring revenue drops below target, when customer acquisition costs exceed profitable thresholds, when inventory levels suggest potential stockouts or overstock situations, or when key customers show signs of payment distress. These alerts help you maintain situational awareness without constantly monitoring dashboards or waiting for monthly reports.

Reducing Costs Without Cutting Staff

One of AI's most immediate benefits is eliminating time-consuming manual tasks that add little strategic value. This doesn't necessarily mean reducing headcount—it means redeploying your team to higher-value activities that drive growth.

Many finance teams spend hours each week entering data from invoices, receipts and bank statements into accounting systems. AI can automatically capture, categorize and enter this information with accuracy rates exceeding 95%. This automation eliminates errors while freeing your team to focus on analysis and planning. The traditional month-end close process involves numerous manual reconciliations, adjustments and reviews. AI can automate many of these tasks, reducing close time from weeks to days. Faster closes mean earlier insights, allowing you to adjust strategies while they can still impact current-quarter results.

Expense management becomes more intelligent with AI automatically categorizing expenses, flagging policy violations and routing approvals to appropriate managers. This reduces administrative burden while improving compliance and visibility into spending patterns. You'll spot trends and opportunities for cost reduction without manually reviewing every transaction.

Perhaps most importantly, AI excels at pattern recognition, making it highly effective at detecting fraudulent transactions or suspicious activities. It can identify unusual vendor payments, duplicate invoices or unauthorized changes to banking information—catching fraud before significant damage occurs.

Real-World Impact: The Service Company That Saved $50,000

A professional services client discovered that AI expense categorization revealed over $50,000 in annual miscategorized expenses. These misclassifications were causing them to miss legitimate tax deductions and prevented accurate departmental cost analysis. The AI system not only corrected future categorizations but helped them file amended returns to recover missed deductions.

Gaining Competitive Advantages

AI's ability to process vast amounts of data and identify patterns provides insights that would be impossible to discover manually. These insights can become significant competitive advantages when applied strategically.

Customer profitability analysis becomes far more sophisticated with AI analyzing customer data to identify your most and least profitable relationships, taking into account not just gross margins but also service costs, payment terms and growth potential. This analysis helps you focus sales efforts on high-value prospects while addressing issues with unprofitable customers.

The predictive capabilities extend to customer behavior as well. By analyzing payment patterns, order frequencies and communication patterns, AI can predict which customers are likely to increase their purchases, experience payment difficulties, reduce or eliminate orders, or require additional support or services. These predictions enable proactive account management, helping you strengthen relationships with valuable customers while addressing problems before they escalate.

Dynamic pricing optimization becomes possible as AI analyzes market conditions, competitor pricing and customer behavior to recommend optimal pricing strategies. This is particularly valuable for businesses with complex pricing structures or those operating in dynamic markets. AI can also analyze your sales data, market trends and customer feedback to identify expansion opportunities you might not see manually, including new product lines, untapped customer segments or geographic markets with strong potential.

Scaling Without Proportional Cost Increases

As your business grows, traditional finance operations often require proportional increases in staff and systems. AI enables you to handle significantly more transaction volume and complexity without corresponding cost increases.

The scalability advantage is dramatic. AI can process thousands of transactions with the same accuracy and speed as dozens. Whether you're handling 100 or 10,000 monthly invoices, AI systems maintain consistent performance without additional labor costs. This scalability extends to compliance and controls as well. As your business grows, maintaining internal controls becomes more complex and time-consuming. AI can automatically enforce policies, flag exceptions and maintain audit trails—ensuring compliance without manual oversight.

Resource allocation becomes more intelligent as AI analyzes your business patterns to optimize staffing and planning. For example, it might identify that certain customers require more support during specific seasons, allowing you to plan accordingly. The standardization that comes naturally with AI enforcement of consistent processes becomes increasingly valuable as you add locations, product lines or customer segments, ensuring that growth doesn't lead to operational drift or control weaknesses.

When AI Makes Financial Sense for Your Business

Not every business is ready for AI implementation, and timing matters. Understanding when AI investment makes sense helps you avoid premature adoption while ensuring you don't fall behind competitors.

Based on our experience with hundreds of businesses, AI typically delivers positive ROI when annual revenue exceeds $2-3 million, monthly transaction volume exceeds 500 items, you have multiple revenue streams or customer segments, manual processes consume more than 20 hours per week, or financial reporting takes longer than one week to complete.

The cost-benefit analysis has become increasingly favorable as AI implementation costs have decreased dramatically. Many solutions are now available for less than the cost of hiring additional staff. Consider AI when the monthly cost is less than 50% of hiring equivalent staff, the payback period is under 12 months, the solution integrates with your existing systems, and implementation doesn't require significant IT resources.

Certain indicators suggest your business would benefit from AI automation: frequent errors in financial reporting or data entry, difficulty meeting month-end close deadlines, limited visibility into business performance between reporting periods, customer complaints about billing or payment processing, or inability to analyze profitability by customer or product line.

Well-implemented AI solutions typically deliver a 30-50% reduction in manual processing time, 15-25% faster month-end close, 90%+ reduction in data entry errors, 20-40% improvement in cash flow prediction accuracy, and 10-20% cost savings through process optimization.

Practical Implementation Strategy

Implementing AI doesn't require a complete system overhaul. The most successful approaches start small, prove value and expand gradually.

Begin with processes that are highly manual and time-consuming, prone to errors or inconsistencies, not mission-critical to daily operations, and well-documented and standardized. Common starting points include expense categorization, invoice processing and basic reconciliations.

Choose one process for a 30-60 day pilot program. This allows you to test the technology with real data, train your team on new processes, measure actual vs. projected benefits, identify implementation challenges, and build confidence before broader adoption. Ensure any AI solution integrates seamlessly with your current accounting and business systems.

Avoid solutions that require significant changes to your established processes or create data silos.

AI should augment human decision-making, not replace it entirely. Maintain appropriate oversight and review processes, especially for large or unusual transactions, customer payment disputes, vendor setup and changes, and financial reporting and analysis.

Prepare your team for AI implementation by explaining how AI will make their jobs easier and more strategic, providing adequate training on new processes, addressing concerns about job security, and celebrating early wins and improvements.

Implementation Success: The Distribution Company's Gradual Approach

A distribution company with $15 million in revenue started with AI-powered invoice processing for their 200+ monthly vendor invoices. After achieving 90% automation within 60 days, they expanded to customer billing and then inventory management. Over 18 months, they reduced their finance team's manual work by 40% while improving accuracy and speed. The freed-up time allowed them to implement monthly customer profitability analysis and weekly cash flow forecasting—capabilities they never had resources for previously.

Managing Risks and Maintaining Controls

While AI offers significant benefits, implementation requires attention to risk management and internal controls.

AI systems process sensitive financial data, making security paramount. Ensure any solution provides bank-level encryption for data transmission and storage, role-based access controls, regular security audits and compliance certifications, and clear data ownership and portability guarantees.

Maintain detailed records of AI decisions and processes for audit purposes. This includes documentation of AI logic and decision criteria, records of human review and override decisions, backup of original source documents, and clear accountability for AI-generated transactions.

Modify your internal control procedures to account for AI automation by defining approval thresholds for AI-generated transactions, establishing review procedures for automated decisions, creating exception handling processes, and updating segregation of duties documentation.

When selecting AI vendors, evaluate their financial stability and business longevity, customer references and case studies, integration capabilities and support quality, data security practices and compliance certifications, and contract terms for data ownership and termination.

Looking Forward: The Competitive Imperative

AI adoption in finance is accelerating rapidly. Businesses that delay implementation risk falling behind competitors who are already gaining advantages through faster decision-making, reduced costs and better insights.

The question isn't whether your business will eventually use AI—it's whether you'll be an early adopter who gains competitive advantages or a late adopter who struggles to catch up. The technology is mature, costs are reasonable and benefits are measurable.

Consider AI as part of your broader growth strategy. Just as you've invested in financial infrastructure, team development and technology systems, AI represents the next evolution in building a scalable, efficient business.

Start exploring AI solutions now, even if implementation is months away. Understanding the landscape, evaluating vendors and planning integration takes time. The businesses that begin this process today will be best positioned to capitalize on AI's benefits tomorrow.

Key Takeaways

- **AI delivers measurable business results.** Focus on solutions that reduce costs, accelerate decision-making and provide competitive advantages rather than just automating existing processes.

- **Start small and scale gradually.** Begin with high-impact, low-risk applications like expense processing or invoice automation before expanding to more complex areas.

- **Timing matters, but don't wait too long.** AI typically delivers positive ROI for businesses with $2-3 million+ in revenue and sufficient transaction volume to justify automation.

- **Integration is crucial.** Choose solutions that work with your existing systems and processes rather than requiring complete overhauls.

- **Maintain human oversight.** AI should augment human decision-making, not replace it entirely. Keep appropriate controls and review processes in place.

- **Think strategically about competitive advantage.** Early AI adopters will have significant advantages in speed, insight and efficiency over businesses that delay implementation.

AI in finance isn't about replacing your team—it's about empowering them to focus on strategic activities that drive growth while automating routine tasks that consume valuable time. The businesses that embrace this transformation thoughtfully will be best positioned for sustainable growth and competitive success.

CEO Confidence Quiz

A s the leader of a growing business, you're keenly aware that the success of your company hinges on your ability to make financially sound business decisions. In other words, in addition to being your organization's visionary, your team is counting on you to assess their proposals and approve those that will enhance your ability to compete at a reasonable cost. But without the right information at your fingertips, it's impossible to make such decisions with confidence.

The following quiz was created to shed some light on your readiness for making important financial decisions. It's based on real questions from real companies with whom I have worked over the past decade to provide strategic financial advice and tactical support. It will help you determine if you and your team are financial wizards or if you have crucial gaps in your knowledge that are inhibiting your ability to thrive.

Answer the questions and total the number of "Yes" answers. Then, use the key to see how ready you are.

In the end, we hope you find this quiz illuminating and the answers useful toward assessing your firm's financial confidence. As always, you're welcome to contact me at william@tcrh.co to discuss any questions that arise.

The Quiz

Instructions: Read through each question and answer Yes or No. As a second mental step, ask yourself if you know where in your financial data or other reports you would look to find the data required to support your answer in a real-world scenario. If you feel confident, check Yes. Sum your number of Yes answers at the bottom of the quiz. If you answer No to a question, read through our advice for how to arrive at a "Yes" in the following pages.

YES   NO

01. Are you confident in your ability to fund your business for the next 6-12 months?

02. Do you know how to increase cash flow for your business?

03. Do you know how much capital you need for the next 12 months?

04. Does your team have the expertise you require to raise capital?

05. Are you confident that you can sell potential investors on your vision?

06. Do you have an idea as to how much your company is worth?

07. Do you know the key performance indicators (KPIs) for your company?

08. Are your financial reports insightful enough to guide your decisions?

09. Do you have a financial forecast that provides clear visibility into the next 12 months?

10. Does your finance and accounting staff have the skills you need to take your business to the next level?

11. Do you have either a part-time or full-time CFO on your team?

Total "Yes" Answers ▶

Answer Key

0-2	3-5	6-9	10-11
UH-OH	**Good Start, But...**	**Getting there!**	**You're a wizard!**
Yikes! Contact us ASAP - if this continues, you might find your business in trouble soon (if it's not already).	You've got some work to do! If you can't tackle it alone, feel free to call us for a free consultation.	You're doing well, but you may have a few blind spots. Contact us the next time you have a financial puzzle you can't solve.	Why are you taking this quiz?! Clearly, you've got everything under control. Carry on with confidence!

How to Read a Profit and Loss Statement

E very business leader who must assess a company's financial performance and make decisions should know how to read a profit and loss statement. Yet, as a fractional Chief Financial Officer (CFO) who works closely with leadership teams, I have noticed that many do not receive this training. Although I'm happy to educate clients on the basics, everyone could benefit from this knowledge. Below, I explain the purpose of the profit and loss (P&L) report, its essential components and how to analyze a P&L statement to unearth valuable insights.

What is a Profit and Loss Statement?

A profit and loss statement (a.k.a. P&L statement or income statement) is a financial document showing how your organization generated and spent money to produce a profit (or loss) over a specific period of time. Put differently, the P&L explains how your revenue and expenses contributed to your company's financial health.

Profit and loss statements are one of three core financial reports business leaders use to monitor a company's economic performance. The other two financial statements are the balance sheet (a tally of assets and liabilities at a specific point in time) and the cash flow statement (a report of how cash has moved in and out of the business over time).

Ideally, your team will produce and review these reports regularly—monthly, quarterly and yearly.

What is the Purpose of a P&L Report?

To run a financially viable business and make informed decisions, you must know:

- How much money is coming into the business (your income)
- How much money is going out (in the form of the cost of revenue and operating expenses)
- How this activity affects your bottom line

That is the primary purpose of a P&L statement. If the data behind the report is sound and meets accounting conventions, you can assume you are profitable if you generate more money than you spend. If the inverse is true, you are running the business at a loss.

However, that is only part of the story. The magic happens when you and your leadership team set goals and then use the data in your P&L statements (and other reports) to track trends and forecast the future. That gives you the insights you need to strategically guide your growing organization, spotting and addressing problems before they spin out of control.

Profit and loss statements are also necessary for communicating with stakeholders. For example, when you file your taxes, the IRS will expect an abridged copy of this report. Lenders, investors and significant customers will also ask for this information.

Of course, no one expects you to prepare these reports alone. Most CEOs hire a Chief Financial Officer (CFO) or a fractional CFO to own this business function. The CFO ensures the numbers behind the reports are accurate and then analyzes them to develop insights and recommendations. That said, understanding the basics will make these discussions more productive.

How to Read a P&L Statement Step-by-Step

Profit and loss statements present financial information logically, organized into components with subtotals. Here is the basic flow.

- Revenues
- Costs of Revenues

- Gross Profit (revenues minus cost of revenues)
- Operating Expenses
- Operating Income (gross profit minus operating expenses)
- Other Income and Expenses
- Net Income (operating income minus other expenses)

Your P&L may look slightly different, depending on your industry and the maturity of your accounting function. For instance, if you run a small business with little accounting oversight, your expenses might appear under just one of these areas—a situation I suggest remedying for better insights. Also, consider the following tips before reviewing the numbers on a P&L.

Tip 1: Financial Notes

Reading a P&L statement without context can be challenging. If you are looking at a P&L for a company you don't know, review any notes included with the report or consider obtaining additional information from a company like Dun & Bradstreet. For instance, the notes might explain certain events or the company's accounting practices, which will help you understand the nuances.

Tip 2: Accrual vs. Cash-Based Accounting

It is crucial to know whether the company uses accrual or cash-based accounting. Accrual-based accounting is when you recognize (record) revenue and the associated expenses when earned or incurred (i.e., when the product or service is delivered, or you incur a cost). That differs from cash-based accounting, where you recognize (record) revenues and expenses when you receive or distribute cash. Although this distinction may seem minor, and many small companies can get along just fine with cash-based accounting for a while, it is incredibly impactful for the following reasons.

Accrual-based accounting allows you to monitor revenues and expenses resulting from the same activity in the same time period. That makes it possible to compare apples to apples and glean better insights. Lenders and investors typically request accrual-based records, not cash-based records, for better visibility into your company's financial health. For these reasons, we typically recommend that our cash-based clients switch to accrual-based accounting as soon as possible.

With that in mind, here's what you will find in each section of the P&L report.

Revenues

We typically divide total revenue (sales) data into multiple line items, one for each source. For example, companies selling products and services should separate their sales figures into two high-level "product" and "service" buckets, then break them down further into individual product lines and service types for analysis and benchmarking.

Cost of Revenues

After revenues, is "cost of revenues" (a.k.a. cost of sales) or "cost of goods sold" (COGS). These are expenses directly related to delivering your services or producing your products. Service-based costs include employee salaries and related benefits for those directly servicing customers ("the fee earners"), subcontractor costs, client-related travel, etc. Product-based costs include the raw materials, labor, etc., related to making products.

Operating Expenses

Operating expenses are the day-to-day operational costs necessary for your business to function that are not directly related to producing your products or services. Sometimes referred to as "OpEx" or Overheads, this category includes sales and marketing costs, owner compensation and general and administrative expenses like rent, insurance and payroll.

Like revenues, carefully tracking and categorizing these expenses is essential for valuable insights. You can use this information to manage your budget, track the ROI on specific investments, benchmark against other firms and share details with external stakeholders.

Other Income and Expenses

Expenses or income not falling into the two categories above will appear here. This section can contain many different types of costs or revenues that may not be recurring, so again, categorization is vital. For instance, profit from selling equipment, interest expenses, bad debt, income tax, or "special project" costs will fall under other income and expenses.

Net Income

Of course, you will find net income at the bottom of the P&L report; this is the profit or loss after subtracting the total expenses. To arrive at your net profit margin, divide net income by your total sales.

What is EBITDA?

Some companies also show EBITDA on their P&L statements. EBITDA (Earnings Before Interest, Tax, Depreciation and Amortization) is a commonly used measure of business performance. It is essential because it provides a clear picture of operational profitability across companies with different capital structures and tax rates.

EBITDA also helps to establish a company's valuation, which is why you will hear that the company sold for 4x or 5x EBITDA. However, Generally Accepted Accounting Principles (GAAP) does not define this figure, so its composition can vary from industry to industry.

There are several ways to measure company profitability, not just EBITDA, so it is vital to understand the nuances of whichever figure you choose to view or quote.

Given this context, please review the example P&L statement below to confirm your understanding before pressing forward.

Acme Services, LLC
Profit and Loss
Latest 12 Months

	LTM ended 2/28 (CY)	% of Revenues	LTM ended 2/28 (PY)	% of Revenues	$ Change	% Change
Income						
Consulting Services	3.998.458	84.5%	3.180.662	87.6%	817.795	25.7%
Add'l Services	624.503	13.2%	253.899	7.0%	370.605	146.0%
Products	110.500	2.3%	118.136	3.3%	(7.636)	-6.5%
Other Revenue	14.473	0.3%	81.825	2.3%	(67.352)	-82.3%
Sales Discounts	(17.410)	-0.4%	(4.438)	-0.1%	(12.972)	-292.3%
Total Income	4.730.524	100.0%	3.630.085	100.0%	1.100.439	30.3%
Cost of Goods Sold						
Consulting/Project Related Costs	1.080.370	22.8%	1.225.192	33.8%	(144.822)	-11.8%
Add'l Service Costs	5.000	0.1%		0.0%	5.000	
Products - Costs	294.412	6.2%	100.583	2.8%	193.828	192.7%
Other Costs	77.972	1.6%	24.477	0.7%	53.495	218.6%
Total Cost of Goods Sold	1.457.753	30.8%	1.350.252	37.2%	107.501	8.0%
Gross Profit ($)	3.272.771	69.2%	2.279.833	62.8%	992.938	43.6%
Expenses						
Salary & Commissions	1.466.910	31.0%	1.050.005	28.9%	416.904	39.7%
Advertising & Marketing	244.161	5.2%	47.802	1.3%	196.359	410.8%
Business Development	122.206	2.6%	37.409	1.0%	84.798	226.7%
Research & Development	36.201	0.8%	49.875	1.4%	(13.674)	-27.4%
General Administrative Expenses	771.867	16.3%	394.310	10.9%	377.557	95.8%
Professional Development		0.0%	1.500	0.0%	(1.500)	-100.0%
Amortization Expense	43.066	0.9%	64.600	1.8%	(21.534)	-33.3%
Total Expenses	2.684.411	56.7%	1.645.501	45.3%	1.038.911	63.1%
Net Operating Income	588.360	12.4%	634.332	17.5%	(45.973)	-7.2%
Other Income						
Interest Income		0.0%	5.000	0.1%	(5.000)	-100.0%
Legal Settlement		0.0%	131.235	3.6%	(131.235)	-100.0%
Other Miscellaneous Income		0.0%	(69.031)	-1.9%	69.031	100.0%
Total Other Income	-		67.204		(67.204)	-100.0%
Total Other Expenses	198.227	4.2%	14.895	0.4%	183.332	1230.8%
Net Other Income	(198.227)	-4.2%	52.309	1.4%	(250.536)	-479.0%
Net Income	390.133	8.2%	686.642	18.9%	(296.509)	-43.2%

Profit and Loss Statement Example

How to Analyze a Profit and Loss Statement

Once you understand the components of a P&L and how they come together to present the whole picture, it becomes easier to perform an analysis. You can look at this data in two ways—vertically or horizontally.

A vertical analysis involves showing each cost line as a percentage of the company's revenue and then examining the figures from top to bottom to see how they relate to each other and industry benchmarks. A horizontal P&L statement analysis examines how each figure (including the percentages) changes over time (i.e., the trends) and how that might evolve if your trajectory continues.

To perform a good analysis, you must look at the numbers both ways, asking questions like the following for each area.

Given my perspective, what do these numbers mean for me? In other words, I typically review P&Ls from a business owner's perspective. CEOs want to know if the company will reach its goals, where efficiency opportunities lie and whether they can afford specific initiatives. However, if you are a prospective investor, lender, or customer considering doing business with the company, you will examine the P&L differently.

- Is the figure in question above or below industry norms?
- Is the figure increasing or decreasing over time?
- If this figure differs from what you expected, given the company's goals, industry norms, or other comparisons, can you determine why?
- How might the company resolve the situation? For example, if costs are too high, it could charge more, implement cost-cutting measures, or both.

Let's dig into key figures to show you what I mean.

Revenue

Ideally, a company's revenue numbers will show a smooth upward trajectory over time, not significant swings up and down. That indicates that the company is growing in a controlled and predictable fashion. However, we don't live in a perfect world, so there will be differences depending on the industry, growth stage, business activities, etc. Therefore, you must dig into the details.

For example, where are any changes in these numbers coming from, and how have those changes evolved? They may stem from a specific region, product line, business unit, or customer segment. If one area grew as a percentage of overall revenues while another shrank, that can help you pinpoint opportunities and threats.

You can also look vertically at the company's balance sheet or cash flow statement for clues. If a positive change occurred, was it the result of a product launch, an investment in marketing, or something else?

Gross Profit Margin (Gross Profit / Revenue = X%)

Gross margin is essential because it helps you see how much money the firm makes as a direct result of selling its products and services after subtracting the cost of revenue or COGS but before other expenses. In other words, this is an efficiency measure you can track over time to answer most of the questions above.

However, once again, you must look behind the figures on the page. For instance, if you are reading the P&L statement for a retail or manufacturing company, how do they value the inventory that appears in their cost figures (FIFO or weighted average)? Or, if you are looking at a service-based firm, what do they charge for an hour of labor? What are their "billable" vs. "non-billable" hours? No one can bill for all their time, so reviewing this information can help you understand what is happening.

Operating Margin (Operating Income / Revenue = X%)

The operating margin ratio looks at how much the company has made after accounting for all the costs of running the company (the overheads), including those not directly related to producing products and services but before taxes, interest, etc. That includes sales and marketing costs, research and development costs and general overhead.

Generally, a high operating margin means the business is running efficiently. However, it is essential to compare this figure to industry benchmarks—a retail business will have a very different operating margin than a manufacturing business. Also, as always, look at how the number has changed over time.

For example, suppose your operating margin decreased in one period because you made a significant investment in marketing. That might be okay if the company's revenue figures rise in subsequent periods, especially if the costs are variable and likely to stabilize as the business achieves economies of scale. Likewise, if the company has many capital assets depreciating over time, this figure may be low for a while but increase later once the capital assets become fully depreciated.

The Bottom Line

Learning how to read a P&L report is valuable for CEOs because it empowers you with the knowledge necessary to do so confidently. However, this isn't a skill you can develop overnight. Continue to practice and reach out to a finance expert for additional help.

Cash vs. Accrual Accounting – Understanding the Difference

As a small business CEO, understanding the fundamental accounting methods available to your company is crucial for making informed financial decisions. The two primary accounting methods—cash and accrual—differ significantly in how they record revenue and expenses. Your choice can substantially impact how you perceive your business's financial health. This appendix explains both methods, their benefits and limitations and offers guidance on selecting the right approach for your business.

The Fundamental Difference

The core distinction between cash and accrual accounting lies in the timing of when transactions are recorded:

> **Cash-Based Accounting** recognizes revenue when payment is received and expenses when they are paid out. This method only deals with actual money moving in and out of your business, with no recognition of accounts receivable or accounts payable.
>
> **Accrual Accounting** recognizes revenue when it is earned and expenses when they are incurred, regardless of when cash changes hands. This method accounts for future incoming and outgoing cash that has been committed through invoices or bills.

Practical Examples

To better understand how each method works in practice, consider these scenarios:

Revenue Recognition

Cash Method:

You deliver $10,000 worth of products to a customer on April 1, but don't receive payment until May 15. Under the cash method, you would record this $10,000 as May revenue, since that's when you actually received the money.

Accrual Method:

In the same scenario, you would record the $10,000 as April revenue, at the time you delivered the products and earned the revenue—regardless of when the customer pays you.

Expense Recognition

Cash Method:

You receive inventory and an invoice for $5,000 from a supplier on April 15, but don't pay the bill until May 10. Under the cash method, you would record this $5,000 as a May expense, when the cash actually left your account.

Accrual Method:

In the same scenario, you would record the $5,000 as an April expense, at the time you received the inventory and incurred the obligation—regardless of when you actually pay the supplier.

Advantages and Disadvantages

Cash-Based Accounting

Advantages:

- **Simplicity:** Easier to maintain and understand, requiring less accounting expertise and resources
- **Clear cash position:** Provides an immediate view of how much cash is available
- **Tax timing:** Can offer tax advantages by allowing some control over which year income and expenses fall into
- **Reduced complexity:** No need to reflect accounts receivable or accounts payable on the balance sheet

Disadvantages:

- **Distorted financial picture:** May present a misleading view of business profitability, especially if large sales or purchases occur near period ends
- **Limited growth insights:** Difficult to identify sales and profitability trends when payments are irregular
- **Inventory challenges:** Not suitable for businesses with inventory, as it doesn't properly match expenses with related revenue
- **Investor and lender concerns:** May not satisfy external stakeholders who require more comprehensive financial reporting

Accrual Accounting

Advantages:

- **Accurate financial picture:** Provides a more realistic view of income and expenses, better reflecting business performance
- **Better planning:** Helps predict future cash requirements by tracking accounts receivable and payable
- **Inventory matching:** Properly matches expenses with related revenue, particularly important for inventory-based businesses

- **GAAP compliance:** Follows Generally Accepted Accounting Principles, which is typically required for seeking investment or loans
- **Growth management:** Provides clearer insight into business trends regardless of payment timing

Disadvantages:

- **Complexity:** Requires more sophisticated accounting knowledge and potentially additional staff or resources
- **Cash flow blindness:** Doesn't provide an immediate picture of available cash, requiring additional cash flow reporting
- **Potential tax implications:** May require you to pay taxes on revenue before you've actually received payment

Which Method Should You Choose?

While small businesses with annual revenue under $5 million typically have the option to choose either method for tax purposes, several factors should guide your decision:

Consider Cash-Based Accounting If:

- Your business is service based with no inventory
- You operate primarily on a cash basis with immediate payment
- You're a small business with simple operations and limited resources
- You want to minimize accounting complexity and costs
- You don't anticipate seeking external financing in the near future

Consider Accrual Accounting If:

- Your business maintains inventory
- You frequently invoice customers or accept delayed payments
- You have annual revenue exceeding (or approaching) $5 million
- You plan to seek external investment or financing

- You want to make decisions based on a more complete financial picture
- You anticipate significant growth in the coming years

Regulatory Requirements

It's important to note that the IRS requires businesses to use accrual accounting in certain circumstances:

- Annual gross receipts exceed $5 million
- Your business maintains inventory and relies on it for income
- Your company is structured as a C Corporation with gross receipts over $5 million

Even if you use Cash-Based accounting for tax purposes, maintaining parallel accrual-based records for management purposes can provide valuable insights into your company's financial health.

Transitioning Between Methods

Many businesses start with Cash-Based accounting for simplicity, then transition to accrual accounting as they grow. This transition requires careful planning and potentially the assistance of accounting professionals to ensure accurate conversion of historical financial data. The shift typically involves:

1. Recognizing outstanding receivables and payables as of the transition date
2. Adjusting inventory and prepaid expense accounts
3. Potentially amending prior tax returns (with IRS permission)
4. Implementing new accounting procedures and possibly software

The Bottom Line

While Cash-Based accounting may be simpler to implement and maintain, accrual accounting provides a more accurate picture of your business's financial health and performance. As your company grows and seeks to attract investors or lenders, transitioning to accrual accounting becomes increasingly important. Regardless of which method you choose, consistency is key to meaningful financial reporting and analysis.

For most growing businesses, I recommend using accrual accounting or at minimum maintaining supplementary accrual-based records even if you use Cash-Based for tax purposes. This approach provides the most complete financial information for making strategic business decisions while still taking advantage of any applicable tax benefits.

What Is a Month-End Reporting Package and What Should It Contain?

The month-end reporting package from your finance team has always been critical for making business decisions. But whereas a simple income statement, balance sheet and maybe a statement of cash flows used to be enough, today's fast-paced, data-driven environment demands more. In addition to these basic statements, your company's financial leader should track trends, analyze changes and incorporate operational data into timely, accurate and relevant insights to share with you and your leadership team.

To give you a sense of what to expect from your accounting department (and, ultimately, your Chief Financial Officer), below is a primer on month-end reporting, what the package should contain and the steps involved.

What is Month-End Financial Reporting?

In its simplest form, month-end financial reporting involves reconciling your company's monthly transactions to ensure that your records are accurate before you close the books and generate financial statements. But while this may sound relatively straightforward, like balancing a checkbook, the month-end close process for a business can be quite complex due to its scale.

In addition to reviewing all actual and anticipated inflows and outflows of money, your team may also gather updates from other departments on the state of your inventory, sales projections, petty cash, or upcoming investments. Then, ideally, they will combine all this information to develop and deliver comprehensive financial reports and analyses explaining where things stand today, what you can expect going forward and what you can do about it. Of course, some organizations skip that last step and rely on their CEO to draw conclusions, but in our experience, leaving that work to a financial professional is more effective.

What is the Purpose of Month-End Reporting?

Month-end reporting may sound like a lot of work, but it is an essential best practice for every business, especially those that plan to grow and scale. For example, consider the following benefits and how they might affect your business.

End-of-month reports give you and your team the financial information necessary to run the company and make confident decisions. Monthly reporting empowers you with reliable and timely financial data, so you can quickly address issues, pursue opportunities, answer questions from stakeholders and interact with your board. In addition to simply being a better way to run your business, that helps you build trust with constituents. Rigorous end-of-month reports make navigating each season's year-end close easier because you can rely on the accuracy of your data.

Developing the sustainable, scalable practices necessary to empower month-end reporting is a vital part of a robust financial infrastructure that will power your business for years. Companies with outside lenders, like a bank line of credit, require month-end reporting that includes the basic financial statements plus reports specific to those institutions. So, your monthly financial reports have more value than meets the eye because they contribute to your company's overall health in many ways.

What Should Your Month-End Reports Contain?

Month-end reports should undoubtedly include your company's financial statements. But they should also contain operational data, metrics and dashboards that are useful and meaningful for generating insights.

Remember, your company's leaders will use this data to make decisions. For example, a month-end financial report for an ecommerce company might include the following:

Financial Statements

- Income Statement (a.k.a. P&L statement)
- Balance Sheet
- Cash Flow Statement

Margin Analysis by SKU, Customer (for Wholesale), Product Line

Financial Metrics: Average Order Value (AOV)

Sales & Marketing Metrics:

- Click-Through Rates
- Conversion Rates
- Website Traffic

Operational Metrics:

- Number of Repeat Customers
- Inventory Turns

Social Media:

- Number of Followers on Facebook or Instagram. Better yet, the level of engagement and eventual sales.

Depending on the size and complexity of your business, you could have more or fewer metrics to track. In addition, other types of companies, such as manufacturing, business services, SaaS, etc., will have different KPIs unique to those industries. Be careful, though.

The Value of Executive Oversight

Providing helpful information at month-end does not mean overkill with useless data. Although some businesses adopt great dashboards and metrics, others sometimes go to the extreme, producing an overload of information that leads to "analysis paralysis." The ideal financial report will favor efficiency. The executive team should be able to review it in one hour and get a good feel for where the company is, where it is going and where the challenges and opportunities lie.

That is where having a financial leader/advisor, who can guide your team in developing this information, is crucial. A good CFO will insist on accurate, understandable data they can translate into easy-to-consume operational dashboards and metrics. They will review the trends, use them to build or update financial forecasts, then analyze the results so they can interpret them for the management team and recommend the next steps.

How to Prepare and Present a Month-End Reporting Package

Just because the month-end close process is complex doesn't mean it has to be a struggle. A well-run finance team will adopt a clear set of month-end reporting processes and procedures to ensure that month-end closing and reporting activities occur quickly. There is even a standard set of Generally Accepted Accounting Principles (GAAP) to guide this work.

For example, most organizations will break the process down into repeatable steps and involve several people. That allows them to share the workload and check each other's work. So, depending on the structure of your team, the month-end close process may play out as follows:

- The bookkeeper updates your accounts receivable and accounts payable accounts, then compares all journal entries in the general ledger to your records to ensure accuracy.
- An accountant checks the bookkeeper's work, creates any needed accruals, adjusts your variable and fixed asset values and generates financial statements using your accounting software.

- A controller reviews the resulting information, combines it with data from other departments, then submits a preliminary package to your financial leader for analysis.
- Your CFO reviews the trends, asks questions and analyzes the information compared to the company's overall strategy. The CFO develops insights and recommendations to share with the executive management team and may also create variations of the report to share with other stakeholders.

Naturally, the month-end reporting checklist will vary from company to company and evolve as your business matures. For instance, a small-to-mid-sized service-based business with no inventory may have an accountant do most of this work and use a fractional CFO for oversight. A large ecommerce company, however, will likely employ an entire team of clerks, accountants and financial analysts who must collaborate.

Key Takeaways

The month-end reporting package should contain more than just financial statements straight from your accounting system. An excellent package will also include the following:

- Vital operational data for making impactful business decisions.

- Key metrics and dashboards customized to your company and industry.

- Meaningful and consumable insights you can translate into action.

10 Financial Metrics and KPIs Every CEO Should Know

Financial key performance indicators (KPIs) provide vital insight into your company's health and trajectory. While the most relevant metrics for your business will evolve with your growth stage and industry, certain fundamental measures offer essential visibility for every leadership team. This appendix outlines the ten most important financial metrics that should be on every CEO's dashboard.

Understanding Financial Metrics vs. KPIs

Before diving into specific measures, it's important to distinguish between these two related concepts:

Financial Metrics are quantitative measurements derived from your financial statements that provide insight into business performance. They help you understand the economic reality behind your income statement and balance sheet.

Financial KPIs represent the subset of metrics that are most critical to monitoring your company's strategic goals. These high-level indicators should align with your current business priorities and provide early warning signals for potential problems.

The Essential Financial Metrics

1. Annual Revenue Growth Rate

Formula: (Current Year Revenue / Prior Year Revenue – 1) × 100%

This metric reveals how quickly your business is expanding by comparing total revenue to the previous period. While every company tracks raw revenue numbers, the growth rate provides crucial context by showing momentum or deceleration in your business.

For more actionable insights, consider tracking this metric quarterly or monthly to detect changes in market conditions or sales effectiveness more rapidly. For mature businesses, calculating the compound annual growth rate (CAGR) over multiple years can smooth out short-term fluctuations and reveal your sustainable growth trajectory.

2. Annual Gross Margin Growth Rate

Formula: (Current Year Gross Margin / Prior Year Gross Margin – 1) × 100%

While revenue growth shows business expansion, this metric reveals whether your profitability is keeping pace. Gross margin growth should generally track with or exceed revenue growth in a healthy business. Divergence between these metrics often signals pricing pressure, rising input costs, or operational inefficiencies that require attention.

3. Gross Margin as Percentage of Revenue

Formula: (Gross Margin / Revenue) × 100%

This fundamental profitability ratio shows how much of each sales dollar remains after accounting for direct costs of production or service delivery. It reveals your pricing power and operational efficiency at the most basic level.

Industry benchmarks for healthy gross margins vary widely—software companies often maintain margins above 70%, while retailers might operate successfully with margins below 30%. The key is understanding your industry's typical range and tracking improvement trends within your own business.

4. Operating Expense Ratio

Formula: (Operating Expenses / Revenue) × 100%

This metric measures the efficiency of your "back office" operations by showing what percentage of revenue is consumed by selling, general and administrative expenses, R&D and other overhead costs. A decreasing operating expense ratio over time indicates developing economies of scale—the hallmark of a scalable business model.

As your company grows, this ratio should generally decline, showing that you can funnel more business through your existing infrastructure without proportionally increasing costs. If this ratio remains flat or increases during growth periods, it signals potential operational inefficiencies requiring investigation.

5. Operating Cash Flow Margin

Formula: (Operating Cash Flow / Revenue) × 100%

Cash flow—not accounting profit—is the ultimate determinant of business survival and success. This margin shows how effectively your company converts revenue into usable cash, revealing your operational efficiency and working capital management.

Industry benchmarks vary widely, with asset-light businesses like software typically generating higher cash flow margins than capital-intensive industries like manufacturing. Regardless of your industry, maintaining consistency or improving cash flow margins should be a primary financial objective.

6. Net Working Capital to Assets Ratio

Formula: (Current Assets – Current Liabilities) / Total Assets

This liquidity metric reveals what portion of your total assets is available as working capital to fund growth initiatives or distribute to shareholders. A higher ratio generally indicates stronger financial flexibility, though strategic use of short-term debt can sometimes justify a temporarily lower ratio.

Monitoring this metric helps ensure you maintain sufficient liquidity to weather unexpected challenges while not unnecessarily hoarding capital that could be invested in growth opportunities.

7. Revenue Per Employee

Formula: Revenue / Number of Employees

This productivity metric provides a simple yet powerful gauge of operational efficiency. While optimal values vary dramatically by industry—technology companies often exceed $500,000 per employee while service businesses might target $200,000—the trend over time reveals whether your workforce is becoming more or less productive as you scale.

Significant declines in this metric may indicate unnecessary hiring, inefficient processes, or market saturation requiring new growth strategies. Conversely, steady improvements suggest successful operational scaling and potential for margin expansion.

8. Days Sales Outstanding (DSO)

Formula: Average Accounts Receivable / (Revenue × 365)

This metric reveals the average time required to collect payment after making a sale. Extended collection periods tie up working capital and may indicate customer dissatisfaction, ineffective collection processes, or deteriorating customer financial health.

For B2B businesses with standard 30-day payment terms, a DSO between 30–45 days typically represents healthy collection practices.

Significant increases warrant immediate investigation into your billing and collections processes.

9. Days Payable Outstanding (DPO)

Formula: Average Accounts Payable / (COGS / 365)

DPO measures how long your company takes to pay suppliers after purchasing goods or services. The interpretation of this metric is nuanced and industry-specific. In manufacturing, a higher DPO might reflect favorable supplier terms and effective cash management. In professional services, however, extended payment periods could damage contractor relationships and reputation.

The optimal approach is balancing cash conservation with vendor relationship management, using industry benchmarks as guidance while developing your company-specific targets.

10. Asset Turnover

Formula: Revenue / Average Total Assets

This efficiency ratio shows how productively your business deploys its assets to generate revenue. Higher ratios generally indicate more efficient operations, though optimal values vary significantly by industry based on capital intensity.

Service businesses with minimal physical assets naturally achieve higher asset turnover than manufacturing or retail operations with substantial inventories and equipment. The most valuable comparisons are therefore against industry peers and your own historical performance.

Industry-Specific Considerations

While the metrics above provide valuable insights for virtually any business, certain industries benefit from specialized KPIs that address their unique business models:

Ecommerce

- **Average Order Value (AOV):** Total Revenue / Number of Orders
- **Customer Acquisition Cost (CAC):** Total Marketing Expenses / New Customers Acquired
- **Customer Lifetime Value (LTV):** Average Purchase Value × Average Purchase Frequency × Average Customer Lifespan

SaaS and Subscription Businesses

- **Monthly Recurring Revenue (MRR):** Sum of all monthly subscription fees
- **Churn Rate:** (Customers Lost During Period / Total Customers at Start of Period) × 100%
- **LTV:CAC Ratio:** Customer Lifetime Value / Customer Acquisition Cost

Manufacturing

- **Inventory Turns:** Cost of Goods Sold / Average Inventory Value
- **Capacity Utilization:** Actual Output / Maximum Possible Output
- **Defect Rate:** Number of Defective Units / Total Units Produced

Professional Services

- **Billable Utilization Rate:** Billable Hours / Total Available Hours
- **Average Billing Rate:** Total Billable Revenue / Total Billable Hours
- **Project Profitability:** Project Revenue / Project Costs

Implementing Effective Financial KPI Monitoring

To maximize the value of these metrics in your business, follow these implementation steps:

1. **Build a Comprehensive Financial Model:** Establish a detailed spreadsheet that captures historical data and future projections.
2. **Select Your Critical Few KPIs:** Rather than tracking everything, identify the 5–7 metrics most aligned with your current strategic priorities.
3. **Create a Visual Dashboard:** Develop a concise, visual representation of your key metrics that can be updated monthly and shared with leadership.
4. **Establish Review Cadence:** Schedule regular review sessions to analyze trends, identify concerns and adjust strategies accordingly.
5. **Set Clear Targets:** For each KPI, establish specific targets based on industry benchmarks and your strategic goals.
6. **Cascade Accountability:** Ensure each department understands how their activities influence the company's financial KPIs.

Remember that financial metrics provide the most value when viewed as trends over time rather than isolated snapshots. By consistently tracking these indicators and understanding their relationships to one another, you'll develop a nuanced understanding of your business's financial health and identify potential issues before they become critical problems.

As the business landscape evolves and your company grows, periodically reassess your key metrics to ensure they remain aligned with your strategic priorities and provide the insights most critical to your current growth stage.

How to Pitch to Investors

Congratulations if you're ready to pitch to investors! This milestone indicates your business is poised for growth. Even experienced executives get anxious when asking for funding; it's completely normal given what's at stake. Having worked on dozens of investor pitches for my own companies and clients, I've developed strategies to help you succeed, even if pitching takes you out of your comfort zone.

Preparation Is Key

Before scheduling any meetings, ensure you have a solid business plan, reliable financial projections and a compelling pitch deck. Your pitch materials should tell a cohesive story about your business opportunity and why it's worthy of investment.

Strategic Meeting Management

Scheduling Strategy: Start with lower-priority investors to refine your technique before meeting your top prospects. Plan for approximately 30 minutes per session: 5 minutes for greetings, 15 for presentation and 10 for questions. Always know which information is essential if you need to trim your presentation.

Equipment and Environment: For virtual meetings (now the norm), invest in proper equipment—a good camera, lighting and audio. Use Zoom when possible as it's widely familiar to most investors. Create a professional environment free from distractions, and coordinate with household members to maintain quiet during your meetings.

Technical Preparation: Close all unnecessary applications before sharing your screen. Turn off notifications, silence your phone and have any demonstrations or supporting materials ready to access instantly. This prevents awkward transitions or unprofessional interruptions.

Deliver With Confidence

Practice Extensively: Conduct multiple rehearsal sessions, starting with friends and family before moving to stakeholders who can provide critical feedback. Record these sessions to identify areas for improvement. Practice both virtual and in-person delivery formats.

Research Your Audience: Before each meeting, research the investment firm and the specific individuals you'll meet. Review their website, portfolio companies and LinkedIn profiles. This allows you to tailor your pitch to their interests and investment criteria.

Presentation Approach: Begin by establishing rapport—finding common ground creates trust. Confirm the time available at the start of the meeting to respect their schedule. Speak naturally rather than reading from a script. Start with a concise executive summary of your business opportunity, then tell your story with genuine passion.

Remember that you're not just seeking capital—you're looking for a strategic partner who can help take your company to the next level. Make this clear by engaging investors in dialogue about how they might contribute beyond funding.

Effective Follow-Through

As each meeting concludes, clearly establish next steps and timing. Send a prompt thank-you email with your presentation, recording link and any promised materials. If an investor declines, politely ask for feedback to improve your pitch and inquire whether they know other investors who might be a better fit.

Pitching to investors represents the culmination of hard work and the beginning of your company's next growth phase. Channel any anxiety into thorough preparation, then let your confidence and passion carry you through. Your genuine belief in your business will be your most compelling asset.

Exit Planning—Preparing Your Business for Sale

Selling your business represents a significant milestone after years of hard work and investment. While the prospect of a financial windfall is attractive, the process is complex and emotionally challenging. Having guided numerous business owners through successful exits, I can attest that early preparation is the key to achieving optimal outcomes. This appendix outlines a comprehensive approach to exit planning and the business sale process.

When to Start Planning Your Exit

It's never too early to begin thinking about your exit strategy. Ideally, preparation should start 3–5 years before you intend to sell. At minimum, most owners should begin formal preparation about 12 months before initiating the sales process. Early planning allows you to make strategic improvements that can significantly enhance your company's valuation.

The Nine-Step Process to Selling Your Business

Step 1: Strategic Planning and Preparation

The foundation of a successful exit is thorough planning with the right advisors. Consider engaging an M&A advisor or fractional CFO who can provide objective guidance throughout the process. During this critical stage, your advisor will help you:

Conduct a Comprehensive Business Assessment

- Review your products, services and intellectual property
- Analyze your market positioning and competitive advantages
- Evaluate your leadership team, talent depth and company culture
- Assess your client mix, recurring revenue and contractual relationships
- Scrutinize financial statements, forecast models and growth trends
- Examine systems, processes, controls and operational procedures

Clarify Your Personal and Business Goals

- Define your ideal buyer profile (financial vs. strategic)
- Establish your target sale price and acceptable terms
- Articulate your personal plans post-sale
- Determine your desired level of involvement after selling
- Identify your non-negotiable conditions

Develop an Implementation Plan

Your advisor will help you create a detailed plan to address weaknesses and enhance strengths before going to market. This typically includes:

- Specific improvement initiatives with measurable outcomes
- Timeline and resource allocation for each improvement
- Responsibilities and accountabilities for implementation
- Key milestones and decision points

This planning phase generally requires about one month of intensive work, followed by ongoing guidance throughout implementation and the sales process.

Step 2: Creating Value Through Business Improvements

Based on your implementation plan, you'll make targeted improvements to maximize your company's value. These often include:

Financial Performance Enhancement

- Improving profit margins through cost management
- Cleaning up financial statements and ensuring GAAP compliance
- Addressing revenue concentration issues
- Documenting and formalizing financial processes

Operational Optimization

- Standardizing and documenting processes and procedures
- Implementing improved management systems
- Reducing reliance on the owner for day-to-day operations
- Addressing capacity and infrastructure limitations

Strategic Positioning

- Strengthening your competitive advantages
- Expanding your customer base or addressing customer concentration
- Protecting intellectual property and trade secrets
- Developing a compelling growth narrative

Throughout this phase, it's critical to maintain focus on running your business effectively. Many owners become so consumed with exit preparations that they neglect operations, inadvertently damaging the very value they're trying to build. Your advisors should bear the brunt of the preparation work so you can maintain your focus on performance.

Step 3: Assembling Your Deal Team and Going to Market

When you're ready to pursue a sale, you'll need to build an appropriate team of professionals. The composition will vary based on the size of your business:

- **Small businesses** may utilize a business broker to find qualified buyers
- **Middle-market companies** typically need an M&A advisor to identify potential acquirers
- **Larger enterprises** often engage specialized investment bankers with proprietary networks

Your team will create marketing materials, including:

- A teaser document that provides enough information to generate interest without revealing confidential details
- A comprehensive confidential information memorandum (CIM) with detailed business information, financial data and growth forecasts
- Supporting documentation for due diligence

When marketing materials are ready, your advisor will share the teaser with appropriate networks to generate a list of potential buyers. Throughout this process, confidentiality is paramount to protect your business and maintain stability.

Step 4: Buyer Selection and Initial Deal Structuring

After identifying interested parties, you'll:

1. Have prospects sign non-disclosure agreements before receiving detailed information
2. Review and evaluate initial indications of interest
3. Meet with serious potential buyers to assess fit and intentions
4. Receive and negotiate term sheets or letters of intent (LOIs)

A competitive environment with multiple interested buyers typically yields the best results. Your advisor plays a crucial role during this phase by:

- Coaching you on how to present your company effectively
- Helping you evaluate potential buyers' strategic fit and financial capacity
- Negotiating key terms to maximize value and minimize risk
- Managing the competitive dynamic to drive optimal outcomes

It's worth noting that a failed sales process can diminish your company's perceived value in the market, underscoring the importance of thorough preparation and having experienced advisors.

Step 5: Due Diligence

Once you select a buyer and sign a letter of intent, the due diligence process begins. The buyer will conduct a thorough investigation to verify all aspects of your business:

- Financial records and historical performance
- Customer relationships and contracts
- Operational capabilities and infrastructure
- Legal and regulatory compliance
- Technology and intellectual property
- Human resources and organizational structure

Well-prepared companies view due diligence as confirmation of what has already been disclosed rather than a discovery process. Your deal team should anticipate buyer questions and prepare documentation in advance to maintain momentum and minimize disruptions.

Step 6: Legal Documentation

After completing due diligence, attorneys draft the definitive purchase agreement and supporting legal documents. These typically include:

- Terms and conditions of the sale

- Representations and warranties
- Indemnification provisions
- Non-compete and confidentiality agreements
- Employment or consulting agreements (if applicable)
- Closing conditions and requirements

This stage requires careful review and negotiation to protect your interests while moving toward closing. Your M&A advisor and attorney should work closely together to ensure that the business and legal aspects of the transaction align with your goals.

Step 7: Closing the Transaction

The closing represents the culmination of the sales process. Both parties sign the final agreements, funds are transferred, and ownership officially changes hands. While this step may seem straightforward, it can be emotionally challenging for sellers who have built their businesses over many years. Be prepared for a mix of emotions even if you're fully committed to the sale.

Step 8: Post-Closing Integration

After closing, the integration process begins. This phase typically lasts 6–12 months and varies significantly based on the buyer's plans for your business:

- Financial buyers often maintain existing operations while implementing improvements
- Strategic buyers typically integrate your business into their existing operations
- Your involvement during this period will depend on the terms negotiated in your agreement

A successful integration requires clear communication, realistic expectations and a commitment to a smooth transition. Prepare yourself and your team for the inevitable changes that will occur.

Step 9: Earnouts and Equity Rollovers

If your deal includes performance-based payments (earnouts) or equity in the acquiring company (rollovers), you'll need to monitor and manage these components after closing. To protect your interests:

- Ensure the earnout metrics are clearly defined and measurable
- Understand how control decisions might impact your earnout
- Document how disputes will be resolved
- Set realistic expectations about the likelihood of achieving maximum payouts

Key Factors for a Successful Exit

From my experience guiding business owners through exits, several factors consistently contribute to successful outcomes:

1. **Start early** – Begin preparation years before you intend to sell
2. **Assemble the right team** – Experienced advisors are invaluable throughout the process
3. **Focus on value creation** – Identify and address issues that could diminish your valuation
4. **Maintain business performance** – Don't let exit planning distract from running your business effectively
5. **Know your goals** – Be clear about what you want financially and personally from the sale
6. **Create a competitive environment** – Multiple interested buyers typically yield better terms
7. **Prepare for emotional challenges** – The process of letting go can be difficult even when you're ready
8. **Structure for certainty** – Aim to receive as much value as possible at closing to minimize future risks

Final Thoughts

Selling your business is likely to be one of the most significant financial transactions of your life. With proper planning, expert guidance and realistic expectations, you can navigate this complex process successfully and achieve the outcome you desire. The time and resources invested in preparation will pay dividends in the form of a higher valuation, better terms and a smoother transition.

GLOSSARY

General Accounting Terms

Accrual Accounting: An accounting method that records revenues and expenses when they are earned or incurred, regardless of when cash is exchanged. This method gives a more accurate picture of a company's financial health by matching revenues with the expenses incurred to generate them.

Accounts Payable (AP): Money owed by a business to its suppliers or vendors for goods or services received. These are short-term debt obligations that must be paid to avoid default.

Accounts Receivable (AR): Money owed to a business by its customers for goods or services delivered but not yet paid for. This represents a current asset on the balance sheet.

Annual Report: A comprehensive report on a company's activities and financial performance throughout the preceding year. It provides shareholders and other interested parties with information about the company's financial health and future direction.

Asset: Any resource owned or controlled by a business that has economic value and can be measured in monetary terms. Assets can be tangible (like equipment) or intangible (like patents).

Balance Sheet: A financial statement that provides a snapshot of what a company owns (assets), what it owes (liabilities), and the difference between the two (equity) at a specific point in time. This document shows the company's financial position.

Bookkeeping: The process of recording all financial transactions of a business. It provides the data from which financial statements are prepared.

Cash Accounting: An accounting method that records revenue when cash is received and expenses when they are paid. This method is simpler than accrual accounting but may not accurately represent a company's financial position.

Cash Flow: The net amount of cash moving in and out of a business during a specific period. Positive cash flow indicates more money coming in than going out.

Cash Flow Statement: A financial statement that shows how changes in balance sheet accounts and income affect cash and cash equivalents. It breaks down the analysis into operating, investing, and financing activities.

Chart of Accounts: A structured list of all accounts used by a company to record financial transactions in its general ledger. It serves as the foundation for the accounting system.

Cost of Goods Sold (COGS): The direct costs attributable to the production of goods sold by a company. This includes material and labor costs directly tied to product creation but excludes indirect expenses like distribution and sales force costs.

Depreciation: The allocation of the cost of a tangible asset over its useful life. This accounting method recognizes that assets lose value over time due to use, wear and tear, or obsolescence.

EBITDA (Earnings Before Interest, Taxes, Depreciation, and Amortization): A measure of a company's overall financial performance that removes the effects of financing and accounting decisions. It's often used as a proxy for cash flow generated by operations.

Equity: The ownership interest in a company's assets after deducting liabilities. For a sole proprietorship, equity represents the owner's investment plus accumulated profits or minus losses.

Expense: The cost of resources consumed or services used in the process of generating revenue. Expenses reduce owner's equity and are recognized when incurred, regardless of when cash is paid.

Financial Statement: Documents that summarize a company's financial activities and position. The three main types are the balance sheet, income statement, and cash flow statement.

Fiscal Year: A 12-month period used by a company for accounting purposes that may or may not align with the calendar year. Companies choose their fiscal year to correspond with their natural business cycle.

Fixed Asset: A long-term tangible piece of property that a business owns and uses to produce income and is not expected to be consumed or converted into cash in the normal course of business. Examples include land, buildings, and equipment.

General Ledger: The main accounting record of a business, which uses double-entry bookkeeping and contains all accounts that post to the balance sheet and income statement. It serves as the foundation for preparing financial statements.

Gross Margin: The difference between revenue and cost of goods sold (COGS) expressed as a percentage of revenue. It reveals how much profit a company makes after paying direct costs of producing its products or services.

Gross Profit: The profit a company makes after deducting the costs associated with making and selling its products, or providing its services. It's calculated as revenue minus cost of goods sold.

Income Statement: A financial statement that shows a company's revenues, expenses, and profits or losses over a specific period. Also known as a profit and loss statement (P&L), it indicates a company's profitability.

Inventory: Goods held by a business for sale to customers. Inventory is considered a current asset on the balance sheet.

Journal Entry: The recording of a financial transaction in a journal before it's transferred to the general ledger. Each entry shows which accounts are debited and which are credited.

Liability: A company's financial obligations or debts owed to others. Liabilities appear on the balance sheet and can be short-term (due within one year) or long-term.

Liquidity: The degree to which an asset or security can be quickly bought or sold in the market without affecting its price. Cash is the most liquid asset, while real estate and equipment are considered illiquid.

Net Income: The total earnings of a company after deducting all expenses, taxes, and costs from total revenue. It represents the profit of the business after accounting for all costs of doing business.

Net Worth: The value of all assets minus all liabilities. For a business, this is also known as shareholders' equity or book value.

Operating Expenses: The day-to-day costs a business incurs to keep running, excluding costs directly tied to producing goods or services. Examples include rent, utilities, insurance, and salaries.

Overhead: Ongoing business expenses that are not directly attributed to creating a product or service. These costs are necessary to run the business but are not tied to specific revenue-generating activities.

Profit and Loss Statement (P&L): Another name for the income statement, showing revenues, costs, and expenses during a specific period. It indicates how revenues are transformed into net income.

Retained Earnings: The portion of a company's profits that are kept in the business rather than distributed to shareholders as dividends. These earnings are reinvested in the company or used to reduce debt.

Revenue: The total amount of money generated by a company for selling its goods or services before any costs or expenses are deducted. Also known as sales.

Return on Investment (ROI): A performance measure used to evaluate the efficiency of an investment or to compare the efficiency of several different investments. It's calculated by dividing the benefit (return) of an investment by its cost.

Working Capital: The difference between a company's current assets and current liabilities. It represents the funds available for day-to-day operations of the business.

Financial Ratios and Metrics

Acid-Test Ratio: A more stringent measure of liquidity that divides quick assets (cash, marketable securities, and accounts receivable) by current liabilities. This ratio indicates a company's ability to pay short-term obligations without relying on inventory sales.

Current Ratio: A liquidity ratio that measures a company's ability to pay short-term obligations by dividing current assets by current liabilities. A ratio greater than 1 indicates that the company can pay its short-term debts.

Debt-to-Equity Ratio: A financial ratio indicating the relative proportion of shareholders' equity and debt used to finance a company's assets. Higher ratios indicate more leveraged (higher risk) companies.

Gross Margin Ratio: The percentage of revenue that exceeds the cost of goods sold (COGS). It's calculated by dividing gross profit by revenue and multiplying by 100.

Net Profit Margin: The percentage of revenue remaining after all operating expenses, interest, taxes, and preferred stock dividends have been deducted from a company's total revenue. It measures how much of each dollar of revenue is kept as profit.

Price-to-Earnings (P/E) Ratio: A valuation ratio of a company's current share price compared to its per-share earnings. A high P/E suggests that investors expect higher earnings growth in the future.

Quick Ratio: Similar to the acid-test ratio, it measures a company's ability to use its near-cash assets to extinguish or retire its current liabilities immediately. It's calculated by dividing quick assets by current liabilities.

Return on Assets (ROA): A profitability ratio that indicates how well a company is using its assets to generate earnings. It's calculated by dividing net income by total assets.

Return on Equity (ROE): A measure of financial performance calculated by dividing net income by shareholders' equity. ROE measures a corporation's profitability by revealing how much profit a company generates with the money shareholders have invested.

Financing Types and Terms

Angel Investor: A high-net-worth individual who provides financial backing for small startups or entrepreneurs, typically in exchange for ownership equity in the company. Angel investments often fill the gap between friends and family funding and venture capital.

Bootstrapping: The process of building a company from personal finances or operating revenues rather than external funding. This approach allows founders to maintain full control of the company.

Bridge Loan: A short-term loan used to meet current obligations before securing permanent financing or removing an existing obligation. It "bridges" the gap between the termination of one loan and the beginning of another.

Capital: Financial assets or the value of financial assets, such as funds held in deposit accounts or funds obtained from special financing sources. In business, capital often refers to the money used to fund operations and purchase assets.

Collateral: Assets pledged by a borrower to secure a loan, which can be seized by the lender if the borrower fails to repay. Common forms of collateral include real estate, inventory, and equipment.

Convertible Note: A short-term debt instrument that converts into equity at a later date, typically during a future funding round. This financing vehicle is popular with early-stage startups because it delays valuation discussions.

Covenant: Conditions in a loan agreement that require the borrower to fulfill certain conditions or refrain from taking specific actions. Covenants protect the lender's interests and serve as early warning signals of financial distress.

Crowdfunding : The practice of funding a project or venture by raising small amounts of money from a large number of people, typically via the Internet. This approach democratizes fundraising by allowing entrepreneurs to access capital from the general public.

Debt Financing: Raising capital by borrowing money that must be repaid with interest. This approach doesn't dilute ownership but creates payment obligations regardless of business performance.

Due Diligence: A comprehensive investigation or audit of a potential investment to confirm all material facts. This process helps investors understand the risks and potential returns of an investment opportunity.

Equity Financing: Raising capital by selling shares of ownership in a company. This approach doesn't create repayment obligations but dilutes the ownership percentage of existing shareholders.

Factoring: A financial transaction where a business sells its accounts receivable to a third party (called a factor) at a discount to raise immediate cash. This approach accelerates cash flow by converting receivables into immediate cash.

Family Office: A private wealth management advisory firm that serves ultra-high-net-worth individuals and families. These organizations often invest in private companies as part of their portfolio diversification strategy.

Initial Public Offering (IPO): The process of offering shares of a private corporation to the public in a new stock issuance. An IPO allows a company to raise equity capital from public investors and create a public market for its shares.

Leveraged Buyout (LBO): The acquisition of a company using a significant amount of borrowed money to meet the cost of acquisition. The assets of the acquired company often serve as collateral for the loans.

Line of Credit: An arrangement between a financial institution and a customer that establishes a maximum loan balance that the lender permits the borrower to access. Unlike a conventional loan, the borrower can access funds as needed, up to the maximum amount.

Mezzanine Debt: A hybrid form of financing that combines elements of debt and equity, typically in the form of subordinated debt or preferred stock with fixed returns. This financing type typically sits between senior debt and equity in the capital structure.

Preferred Equity: A class of ownership in a corporation that has a higher claim on assets and earnings than common stock. Preferred shareholders generally receive fixed dividends and have priority over common shareholders in case of liquidation.

Private Equity: Capital investment made into companies that are not publicly traded on a stock exchange. Private equity investors often take controlling stakes in companies with the goal of improving operations and eventually selling at a profit.

Revenue-Based Financing: A type of funding where investors provide capital to a company in exchange for a percentage of ongoing gross revenues. This approach aligns investor returns with company growth without requiring ownership dilution.

SAFE (Simple Agreement for Future Equity): A financing instrument developed by Y Combinator that gives investors the right to receive equity in a future financing round. SAFEs are intended to be simpler than convertible notes, without interest rates or maturity dates.

Seed Funding: The initial capital used to start a business, typically coming from the founders themselves, friends and family, or angel investors. This funding helps support initial product development and market testing.

Senior Debt: Loans or bonds that have the highest priority claim on a company's assets and must be repaid first in the event of bankruptcy. Senior debt typically carries lower interest rates due to its reduced risk.

Series A, B, C Funding: Sequential rounds of venture capital financing, with Series A typically being the first significant round of venture capital investment after seed funding. Each subsequent round (B, C, etc.) generally involves larger amounts of capital at higher valuations.

Term Sheet: A non-binding agreement setting forth the basic terms and conditions under which an investment will be made. This document serves as a template to develop more detailed legal documents for the final agreement.

Venture Capital: A form of private equity provided by firms or funds to startups, early-stage, and emerging companies that have high growth potential. Venture capitalists typically take significant equity stakes and actively participate in the company's development.

Warrants: Securities that give the holder the right, but not the obligation, to purchase a company's stock at a specific price and time. Warrants are often attached to debt instruments as a sweetener for investors.

Tax and Regulatory Terms

Audit: A systematic examination of financial records to ensure accuracy, compliance with tax laws, and adherence to accounting standards. Audits can be conducted internally or by external parties like accounting firms or tax authorities.

Capital Gains Tax: A tax on the profit realized from the sale of a non-inventory asset like stocks, bonds, or real estate. The tax rate varies based on the holding period (short-term vs. long-term) and the taxpayer's income level.

Corporate Tax Rate: The percentage of a corporation's income that is paid to federal, state, and local governments. Corporate tax rates vary by jurisdiction and can be influenced by various deductions and credits.

Deduction: An expense that can be subtracted from gross income to reduce taxable income and therefore the amount of tax owed. Common business deductions include operating expenses, interest payments, and depreciation.

GAAP (Generally Accepted Accounting Principles): The standard framework of guidelines for financial accounting in the United States. GAAP includes standards, conventions, and rules accountants follow in recording and summarizing transactions and preparing financial statements.

IFRS (International Financial Reporting Standards): A set of accounting standards developed by the International Accounting Standards Board (IASB) that is becoming the global standard for the preparation of public company financial statements. IFRS is used in many countries outside the United States.

Qualified Small Business Stock (QSBS): A type of stock that, if held for more than five years, may qualify for reduced capital gains tax rates or even tax exclusion under Section 1202 of the Internal Revenue Code. This provision encourages investment in small businesses.

SEC (Securities and Exchange Commission): The U.S. government agency responsible for regulating the securities industry, stock exchanges, and enforcing federal securities laws. Public companies must comply with SEC disclosure requirements.

Tax Credit: A dollar-for-dollar reduction in the amount of tax owed, as opposed to a deduction which reduces the amount of income subject to tax. Tax credits are more valuable than equivalent deductions because they directly reduce tax liability.

Write-Off: A reduction in the value of an asset or earnings by the amount of an expense or loss. In taxation, a write-off is when an asset's value is recognized as an expense or loss for the purposes of reducing taxable income.